# The Big Green Book

*25 multi-purpose outlines*
*for pre-school groups*

First published 2003. Reprinted 2006, 2007, 2012, 2015

ISBN 978 1 85999 695 9

Scripture Union, 207–209 Queensway, Bletchley, MK2 2EB, England.

Email: info@scriptureunion.org.uk

Scripture Union is an international Christian charity working with churches in more than 130 countries.

Thank you for purchasing this book. Any profits from this book support SU in England and Wales to bring the good news of Jesus Christ to children, young people and families and to enable them to meet God through the Bible and prayer.

Find out more about our work and how you can get involved at:

www.scriptureunion.org.uk (England and Wales)

www.suscotland.org.uk (Scotland)

www.suni.co.uk (Northern Ireland)

www.scriptureunion.org (USA)

www.su.org.au (Australia)

**Performing Licence**

Unless otherwise stated, Bible quotations are from the Contemporary English Version © American Bible Society, published by HarperCollins Publishers, with kind permission from the British and Foreign Bible Society.

British Library Cataloguing-in-Publication Data: a catalogue record for this book is available from the British Library.

**Acknowledgements**

Thank you to Christine Orme and Christine Wood for permission to use copyright material from *Splash*, SU 1992.

Some activities are based on material previously published in *Sing, Say and Move*, *Jigsaw*, *Let's join in*, *Let's Praise and Pray*, *Let's Sing and Shout!* and *Let's all clap hands!* © Scripture Union.

Thank you to Diana Turner and Jackie Cray for so much valuable support and constructive comment.

**A note on Music books**

| | |
|---|---|
| JP | Junior Praise (Marshall Pickering) |
| JU | Jump Up If You're Wearing Red (NS/CHP) |
| KS | Kidsource (Kevin Mayhew) |
| GTB | Gospelling to the Beat (Scripture Union Australia) |
| ISLK | Ishmael's Songs for Little Kids, CPO 1999 |

Series Editors: Maggie Barfield, Sarah Mayers

Project Manager: Louise Titley

Editorial support: Lizzie Green

Writers: Judith Wigley, Jackie Harding, Ruth Dell, Geraldine Witcher, Kathleen Crawford, Val Mullally

Additional material: Maggie Barfield, Vicki Barfield, Marjory Francis, Liz Lunn, Denise Niel, Susie Matheson, Janet Meredith, Judith Merrell, Ruth Ranger, Christine Wright

Cover and internal design by Mark Carpenter Design Consultants

Cover photography: Steve Shipman

Illustrations: Claire Vessey

Printed in Malta by Gutenberg Press Ltd

# Contents

# Welcome to Tiddlywinks...

**Remember the game?** Play it anywhere, anytime with almost any age. It can be a two-minute time filler or an afternoon of family fun captivating even the youngest child's attention. Flipping, flying coloured discs, furious scrambles after lost 'winks' and triumphant laughter as three-year-old Lucy beats Grandad again! It's so simple, such fun.

Welcome to *Tiddlywinks*... resource material for young children that's fun, flexible, and extremely user-friendly.

**Fun** because it's child and therefore 'play' centred. The material reflects the understanding that young children grow, develop and learn through play. *Tiddlywinks* provides young children with a wide range of enjoyable, stimulating play experiences as a basis for learning about themselves, the world in which they live and the God who made both them and that world. It's designed to be good fun!

**Flexible** because it is adaptable to almost any situation. The work of the Christian church is no longer restricted to Sundays as literally thousands of carers and their young children flock through the doors of our churches, halls, and community buildings between Monday and Friday. Thankfully church leaders are waking up to the fact that what happens midweek really matters, and these people are being increasingly valued as members of the extended church family. That in no way devalues the very important work that goes on during a Sunday, both within the framework of a service of worship or Sunday teaching group. BOTH Sunday and midweek work are important and of equal value, but material that's easily adaptable to a variety of different

contexts needs to be flexible. *Tiddlywinks* has been written and designed with that flexibility in mind. Whether you are responsible for a midweek carer and toddler group, pram service (more likely to be called something like Butterflies, Minnows or Little Angels!), or you are a leader in a playgroup or nursery class, overseeing a Sunday crèche, teaching an early years Sunday group class, or part of a community based play centre or shoppers' crèche – there is material in *Tiddlywinks* that will be adaptable to your situation. Some of you will be looking to fill a two-hour programme, others two minutes! *Tiddlywinks*' pick-and-mix style is here to meet the needs of a wide range of contexts.

**User-friendly** because it is accessible to leaders who are just starting out as well as those with more experience. Whether you're wondering how to tell a Bible story, wanting to learn age-appropriate rhymes and songs, looking for creative ideas for prayer or wondering how telling the story of Noah might fit in with your early learning goals, *Tiddlywinks* can help you.

*Tiddlywinks* places great importance upon relationships. It recognises the crucial role of parents, carers and leaders in the development of a young child in his or her early years and the need to support and encourage all who share in this important task. Friendship between adults and children creates community, identity and a sense of belonging. When that community becomes a safe place where trust and friendship grow, both adults and children thrive within it. There could be no better foundation in the life of a young child.

## OK, but you still have questions

Each outline has an activity page which can be used either in the group or at home. Photocopy as many pages as you need. Some of the craft activities recommended on these pages will work better if you photocopy them directly onto thin card instead of onto paper. Encourage adults to talk about the leaflets with the children and to do the activities together.

If the sheet is taken home, you could photocopy your group news or notices onto the blank reverse.

Where do I start…? How do I use it…? Who can use it…? Where can it be used…? When is the best time…? Why introduce spiritual topics to young children at all…? Do I need special equipment…? What skills will I need…? Will it cost anything…? Who will come…?

Everyone who has worked with young children has asked these and many other questions at some stage! The writers of *Tiddlywinks* are firmly convinced that adults learn through experience too.

In fact, 'hands-on' is the very best way to learn! No academic or paper qualification can replace first-hand experience of simply being and engaging with young children as they play and learn. The best qualifications for working with young children are a desire to be with them and a willingness to learn.

The following pages are here to help you think through questions you may have, guide your planning and preparation and help you get the best for your children from *Tiddlywinks*. We start with the all-important question WHY? If you are convinced of the reasons for working with young children, developing body, mind and spirit, you will keep going even when it feels tough. Conviction produces commitment and determination, qualities worth cultivating in any children's leader. And *Tiddlywinks* is here to help. Enjoy it!

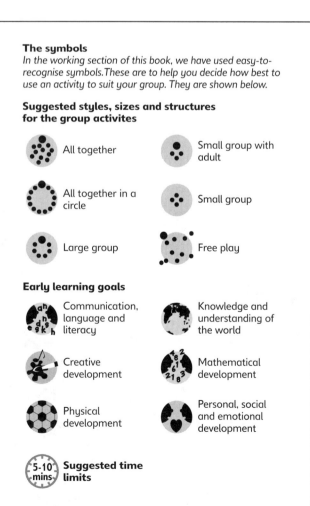

**The symbols**
*In the working section of this book, we have used easy-to-recognise symbols. These are to help you decide how best to use an activity to suit your group. They are shown below.*

**Suggested styles, sizes and structures for the group activites**

All together

Small group with adult

All together in a circle

Small group

Large group

Free play

**Early learning goals**

Communication, language and literacy

Knowledge and understanding of the world

Creative development

Mathematical development

Physical development

Personal, social and emotional development

5-10 mins. **Suggested time limits**

# Why?

**Why** work with babies, toddlers and pre-schoolers? Why go to such lengths to provide appropriate play facilities, resources and materials for such young children? Let's be honest; they are noisy, messy, sometimes smelly, and thoroughly exhausting!

But, as the psalmist reminds us, they are also very special, a gift from God:

*You are the one who put me together
inside my mother's body,
and I praise you
because of the wonderful
          way you created me.*

(Psalm 139:13–14)

Few of us would deny the wonder of a new baby. The sense of miracle is often overwhelming and awe inspiring, and it isn't difficult to believe in a Creator God at such times. But the real truth behind the psalmist's words is that God's mark is upon each and every one of us right from the very beginning. From conception each one is a unique, individual human being, made in the image of God.

God's image within us is spiritual, and children (especially young children), are spiritual beings in their own right. As leaders, parents or carers of young children God gives us the awesome responsibility of sharing in his creation process. As the children in our care grow in body, mind and spirit, we become partners with God in that developmental process. Research tells us that the first five years of a child's life are the most crucial, laying down important foundations for the rest of life. If that is so, we know that we face quite a challenge. The stimulus we provide, the environment in which they grow, the quality of relationships and the values they experience will make an enormous difference to the children in our care.

Good relationships between young children and their carers are crucial for healthy growth and development. A child who experiences love, trust, security and forgiveness in their closest human relationships will quickly understand about the God who also loves, cherishes, protects and forgives them. When they become part of a community that lives out those values the impact is even greater. Their experience will make sense of all they will come to learn through the many Bible stories they hear; stories that reflect those same values and truths. When a group both practices and teaches these values it becomes a powerful place of spiritual learning for all who are part of that community. Young children and their parents and carers will thrive and grow in body, mind and spirit.

When fostered at an early age the relationship between a young child and God is transparently beautiful, often uncomplicated and spontaneous. Children are often more in touch with their spirituality than adults. They sense, they feel, they wonder but don't necessarily express those things in words. Their experience of God doesn't always need words. On several occasions in the Gospels Jesus used children as an illustration of those to whom the kingdom of God belonged encouraging adults to 'become as a child' in order to enter that kingdom (Luke 18:15–17; Mark 10:13–16; Matthew 19:13–15).

Many adults' lives have been greatly influenced by the faith of a child. By sharing in their experiences, teaching them appropriately, guiding them gently, and enabling them to grow in body, mind and spirit they too have come to a greater understanding of God, his relationship with us and plan and purpose for our lives. We live in an age where two, almost three generations of adults have had little or no positive teaching about God or experience of the church. Many of these are the parents of the children in our pre-school groups. Some of us reading these introductory pages (including the writer!) will not have received a Sunday school education but others will have been nurtured in the Christian faith from the cradle. Many of the stories we share with our children will be new to us. The action rhymes and songs of praise may be the first 'hymns' we have ever sung. Many of the ideas for prayer will be our introduction to prayer. It's a whole new journey, one in which our children will undoubtedly lead us, but a journey which, in hindsight, we shall all travel together.

Why share spiritual truths with young children? Because we all want the very best for our children and in seeking to provide the best we are all privileged to learn from them in the process.

# Where and when?

**Where and when** you use *Tiddlywinks* material will vary considerably, as will the extent of the use of the material provided. Each session incorporates different child-centred activities linked by a theme: Play time; Game time; Making time; Story time; Rhyme time; Song time; Pray time. You may be in a position to influence everything that happens in your group and therefore, make use of any number of these. Alternatively you may have responsibility for one part of your group's programme, eg the singing time, a craft activity, or story time. The joy of *Tiddlywinks* is that you can simply extract what you need for use at any one time.

Let's look at the variety of different contexts in which pre-school groups meet and the way in which they might use *Tiddlywinks* material:

## Midweek 'pram' services
*Tiddlywinks* contains all that a leader might need for these short, midweek 'services' of worship for pre-school children. Time may prevent them from using all the material and lack of suitable facilities may restrict the type of Play time and Making time, especially if these groups meet inside the main body of their church (although there are a number of ingenious and creative ways of adapting what might at first seem insurmountable obstacles). But, provided they have an area in which they can move safely and sit comfortably together, Game, Story, Pray, Rhyme and Song time will be ideal for these occasions.

## Midweek parent/carer and toddler groups
These important groups provide a much needed meeting point in the community particularly for first time parents and carers of young children. They are led by a wide range of people, including leaders formally appointed by the church, Christian mums who attend the group with their own children, and mums, or carers, who have little contact with the church but who use (often renting) church buildings as a meeting place. Some will run along very similar lines to pram services seeking to provide a place where Christian values will be experienced and the faith taught. Others, will simply be seeking to provide quality play and creative stimulation for the children present. *Tiddlywinks* material can meet both of these needs with leaders carefully selecting what they feel is appropriate for their situation. Whilst each section is thematically linked it can also stand on its own. Linking a five-minute craft activity with a ten-minute singing time may be all that is required whilst others will incorporate a story and prayer time. It is totally flexible.

## Sunday groups
Many Sunday crèches and early years teaching groups (usually for children aged two-and-a-half to five years) will be looking for a balanced teaching programme to follow over a set number of different weeks, covering the whole of the church's festivals and seasons. These children will generally come from Christian homes and families where the faith is lived as well as taught. *Tiddlywinks* will offer an extensive range of topics and themes ideally suited to this context, and of course the teaching and learning style is always child-centred and age appropriate.

## Playgroups and nurseries
Most playgroups and nurseries for two-and-a-half to five-year-olds are officially registered with OFSTED and seek to follow the early years educational goals and guidelines. Leaders are trained and fully responsible for the children in their care. Whilst not written with the sole intention of meeting the educational requirements of these goals, much of the material will serve to enhance and supplement the curriculum required for these groups.

## Informal settings, eg coffee mornings and drop-in centres
These informal and casual places of meeting provided by many churches regularly attract young children but rarely provide adequate facilities for them. Following five minutes of biscuit munching they are bored and restless. A simple craft activity, a couple of songs and rhymes, and a short story can make their brief visit a very valuable experience. It's a statement about how much we value these children as well as a valuable teaching opportunity. It also encourages them to return.

## Special events
Many churches recognise that what happens on a Sunday morning is often inaccessible and inappropriate to young children and their families. But this does not always mean that there is not an interest in learning about and experiencing the Christian faith. Many groups are experimenting with occasional events geared entirely for young families at a time that is suitable for them. Some have found Saturday tea times a good meeting time, others Sunday afternoons. Festivals, ie Christmas, Easter, Harvest etc are excellent starting points for these and often draw large numbers of people, especially when food is part of the programme. The *Tiddlywinks* special feature (designed for big group events – see pages 90 and 91) and/or *Tiddlywinks* session material can be creatively used to provide a theme base with all the necessary ingredients for an enjoyable family-friendly programme.

# How?

## How?

When setting out to run a group for pre-school children and their carers there are practical things to consider which are essential, others that are recommended and others still that are a bonus. This page outlines all three. It also includes a recommended plan of action for any who might be starting from scratch.

## ESSENTIAL

### Health and safety

Imagine the building to be used for the group as your own home and apply the same levels of health and safety requirements. Check heaters, floor surfaces, furniture, plug sockets, secure entry and exit points, fire exits, toilet and baby changing facilities, kitchen hygiene and safety if serving refreshments. Be aware of the different allergies that could affect children and encourage leaders to attend a First Aid course. Aim for the highest possible standards of health and safety at all times.

### Child Protection

In the UK, the 1989 Children's Act is designed to encourage good practice and safety in all work undertaken with children aged 0–18 years of age, including that in churches. Any church-sponsored group where children remain in the care of leaders for longer than two hours, and which meets more than six times a year, is required to register with the Social Services department of the local authority. Many of our playgroups and nurseries fall into this category, but parent/carer and toddler groups do not need to register, although many choose to notify local authorities of their existence. Where parents and carers remain with their children for the duration of the session they are held responsible for their own children. Each church denomination or network has drawn up its own guidelines for good practice with recommendations for group leaders working in this context. These can be obtained from national headquarters or through regional children's advisers and should be followed carefully in order to maintain the highest of standards possible.

If you are working outside the UK, please check up on the Child Protection legislation for your area.

### Insurance cover

Insurance for pre-school groups should have appropriate and adequate cover. Existing church policies should always be checked. Specialist agencies such as the *Pre-School Learning Alliance* or *Playgroup Network* work with major insurance companies to provide tailor-made packages for pre-school groups.

## RECOMMENDED

### Storage facilities

You can never have enough storage! What might start as one plastic box full of toys and materials will quickly multiply. Borrow, beg, plead and cry for more boxes, shelves, cupboards, and storerooms that are easily accessible; make setting out and clearing away as easy as possible

### Keeping records

The fire service require a written record of all persons in a public building at any time which provides a very useful record of all who have attended. Additional information such as addresses, phone numbers, birth dates help to inform members in the event of unexpected group closure due to bad weather or sickness, and to acknowledge birthdays of children, all of which shows care and concern. Ensure, however, that confidentiality is maintained with all personal details kept on file. In accordance with the Data Protection Act, do not divulge any information to third parties.

A photocopiable registration form can be found on the inside front cover of *Tiddlywinks: The Big Red Book*.

### Teamwork

This work requires storytellers, singers, craft specialists, people who will keep a register, take monies, make refreshments, set out and clear away, etc. Where teamwork is fostered it also becomes a training ground for future leaders: those making coffee may develop into wonderful storytellers, songwriters or craft workers. Try to create an atmosphere where people are free to learn and you will grow your own leaders naturally.

### Budgeting

Much of this work incorporates both the spiritual nurture of children and outreach to carers and families. Many churches allocate a specific amount of budget money for this purpose but don't always recognise the context in which it is being done. Be sure to remind them and ask for ongoing financial support to fund the work. Training leaders, publicity, resource books, craft materials, play equipment, refreshments and various other miscellaneous items can be costly. Keep a record of expenditure and income, with proof of purchases at all times. Don't be worried about making a charge for the group, as many parents/carers are more than willing to contribute towards something that their children enjoy.

## BONUS

### Behind the scene helpers

There are many housebound people in our churches who love to be involved in children's work. Publicity, programmes and newsletters can be designed on computers; craft materials cut and prepared well in advance and prayer can be a vital and encouraging support to a tired and weary leader. A little advance planning can alleviate a lot of pressure when shared with willing home-based workers.

### Outside funding

Occasionally groups have benefited from charitable grants. Different bodies vary considerably in the criteria set out for funding – many decline groups that promote religious activities whilst others seem much more open. Local libraries usually have details of local and national charities.

If starting your group from scratch you should always seek the permission and support of your church leadership body. Go equipped with a well thought through plan of action.

# Playing with a purpose

**Play** is the basis for almost every part of the *Tiddlywinks* material because the writers know and understand that young children learn everything through playing. Their capacity to listen is limited to just one minute for each year of life and so the suggestions offered include very few 'listening only' activities. In recent years educationalists have confirmed that all ages of children and adults learn far more through what they do and experience than simply through what they hear.

Each part of the theme-based *Tiddlywinks* programme is designed to offer young children some kind of play with a purpose. As a child moves from one activity to another, joining in small and large group experiences, he or she is gathering understanding and experience of that topic or theme. Of course some won't make the connections, but others will.

What is most important is that each activity is accessible and meaningful and it is the leader's task to provide the basic ingredients and stimulus for creating the best possible, purposeful play experience. Let's consider the different play sections of the programme:

## Play time

**(unstructured play)**
'Play time' describes a variety of unstructured play activities, many of which will connect with children's every day life and experiences. This is likely to take up the bulk of the session and greet children on arrival. It will help introduce them to the day's topic, eg animals for story of Noah, boats for story of Jesus and the storm, food for story of feeding 5,000 etc, acquire the vocabulary (when stimulated by adults) for use in the songs and rhymes, and explore concepts, eg animal families, effects of water, sharing out food between friends and dolls. All these play experiences are valuable in their own right but also become important foundations in a programme designed to help young children learn about a specific Christian story or Bible truth.

## Game time

**(cooperative play)**
Young children generally play alone but simple, non-competitive games will develop an awareness of others and a sense of belonging to a group. They will learn to share, take turns, watch (and imitate) others, express delight in both their own and others' achievements, and respond to each other. Physically active games also stimulate physical development especially coordination and balance. Games can strengthen relationships within a group and help create a community built on Christian values, as well as provide a greater understanding and experience of the story or theme being developed.

## Story time

**(engaging play)**
When creatively led, a story time demands much more than just listening. Most Bible stories lend themselves to visual, sound and action aids, actively engaging as many of the children's senses as you possibly can. Participation will involve ears, voices, hands (and legs) but also the emotions. Young children will live through the characters they are introduced to, imagining, feeling, sensing, and exploring all aspects of the story you are telling. They may not be able to respond with words but they will be learning.

## Making time

**(creative play)**
Creative play introduces young children to a whole new world. The learning here most definitely takes place in the process of making and not in the end product, even though it will be greatly cherished and a very important reminder of the day's theme or story. Size, shape, texture, colour and patterns are just some of the important discoveries that will be made through making. Children will explore a variety of materials and acquire new skills and techniques. Together parents, carers and children will grow in confidence and creativity; they will uncover the mark of a creative God within them, in whose image they have been made. Whatever the limitations on your space and facilities make 'Making time' possible, as it is one of the most valuable learning experiences of all.

## Song time and Rhyme time

**(musical play)**
Music, rhythm, rhyme and movement are experiences of the womb so it's not surprising that even the youngest of babes will actively respond to this part of the programme. When part of a circle time the learning is far more than simply the words of songs and rhymes being used. Young children learn to listen, follow actions, take turns, recognise each other and be part of a group experience. Even those who appear not to be participating amaze parents by repeating everything they have learnt hours later when at home!

## Adults too

Never underestimate all that adults are learning through the children's play programme. Some are actually learning how to play themselves; others are learning Bible stories and truths for the first time; and others will want to develop that learning through further adult-centred programmes. *Tiddlywinks* even provides suggestions for ways in which you might help them to do so.

# Making the most of structure

**Under-fives** love routine and structure. They learn through rhythm and repetition. It makes them feel secure and safe and helps them to quickly identify people, situations and experiences. As these become positive experiences children will look for them, ask for them and sometimes be very difficult to handle when they don't get them!

Structure doesn't mean boring repetition or inflexibility. It is determined by the basic needs of the children in our care. Every child needs to eat (even if they don't want to!) and so the structure of our day includes several eating times, but, exactly when, where and what we eat is determined by the individual's needs and circumstances. In the same way, a group including young children and their carers needs to have a structure that has been fashioned and shaped to meet the needs and circumstances of its members.

*Tiddlywinks* material is shaped into a structure that incorporates several important components; 'welcome' time; 'circle' time and 'home' time. Each are created to produce familiarity and security for both carers and children.

## Welcome time

Providing a welcome is all about creating a sense of belonging, being part of a community. The key to doing it lies in being ready. Try out the ideas on pages 92 and 93.

## Ready for children

The room or area being used should act like a magnet to every child so that they are immediately drawn into a play activity of some kind. Pre-schoolers are not able to sit around waiting for everyone to arrive! They need to play. When setting out your room make safe provision for babies and early toddlers, keep large pieces of equipment and mobile toys away from activity tables and encourage adult participation by positioning chairs close to activity tables.

## Ready for adults

Establishing eye contact and welcoming individuals by name are the two most important acts of welcome. A one-to-one personal approach helps adults feel they

and their children belong to a caring community. It reflects the love and care that Christians know God has for each individual.

## Ready for newcomers

Newcomers need special treatment. First experiences are lasting ones and once put off they rarely give you a second chance. A leader should be allocated specifically to the task of welcoming new adults and children. Often there are details that need to be taken and procedures to explain which take time. It can also be helpful to provide a little leaflet describing the group, its purpose and structure, giving useful contact numbers.

*Tiddlywinks* provides a number of suggestions for activities that help build a sense of welcome. Remember whatever you choose, it will necessitate you being ready – the most important welcome factor of them all!

## Circle time

Circle time is all about communication, for which you will need to be prepared. It's about preparing any number of the story, rhyme, song and prayer activities suggested in the *Tiddlywinks* material to engage both children and adults within a simple circle. The 'circle' shape is important as it includes everyone and brings them into a position where they can see and join in with what is happening. Participation by everyone is crucial to the success of circle time and many groups choose to go into a separate area or room to avoid distractions of toys and equipment; others simply clear away before starting. This time is key to developing the sense of belonging and group ownership from which will grow shared responsibility and strong community ties.

When you are part of a community you share special occasions together. It may be a birthday (adult's or child's!), special anniversary (of the group or church) or celebration of a newborn baby. Circle time is the ideal time to focus on these special occasions. There may also be sad times for which the group as a whole need to find an expression of shock, grief or sorrow, eg bereavement of a child, a

national tragedy, a local concern. The simple lighting of a candle, a song or prayer may be sensitively incorporated into this special time together.

## Home time

So far, creating our structure has involved being ready and being prepared. Ensuring a positive home time means we have to be organised. Too often under-fives groups simply disintegrate with no positive means of finishing or saying goodbye. People drift away as leaders scurry around tidying up. A positive ending gives a feeling of satisfaction and completion and develops a sense of anticipation for the next meeting.

Many group sessions end with a circle time building in a final song or rhyme that indicates 'this is the end'. *Tiddlywinks* offers a number of different ways in which you can mark the end in this way. Look at the ideas on page 94 and try to choose one that best suits your group, and let it become part of your routine.

# Quick tips to get you started...

**Many** experienced children's leaders find working with groups of young children daunting, especially when parents and carers are present. The skills and confidence required are quite different to those needed to work with older children. If you are new to this age range, or it has been some years since you've had contact with them, spend some time simply being with them and familiarising yourself with their behaviour and play patterns. You will be amazed at how quickly you acquire the knowledge and experience necessary for leading various parts of the *Tiddlywinks* programme. Here are a few tips to get you started:

### ● Using the Bible with young children

Do explain that the Bible is God's very special storybook

Do show the children a child-friendly Bible each time you tell a Bible story so that they become familiar with it

Do make it accessible to them and encourage them to borrow a copy to take home

Don't read straight from the Bible, always 'tell' a story

Do communicate an enthusiasm and excitement for the stories you tell, remembering that you share God's story

Do be prepared for the many questions that some children will ask!

### ● Storytelling

Do make it short (remember one minute of attention for each year of a child's life)

Do sit where you can see and be seen

Do make it visual, eg large pictures, household objects, puppets, Duplo, or toys

Do involve the children in actions, sounds, and repetitive phrases

Do give them time and space to respond to the stories with their comments and questions

Don't be worried about repeating the story, especially if they have enjoyed it!

### ● Leading songs and rhymes

Don't worry about not being able to play an instrument

Do sit at the children's level when leading

Don't teach more than one new song at any one time

Don't pitch songs and rhymes too high or use complex tunes

Do use children's instruments but,

Don't forget to put them away afterwards

Do encourage parents and carers to join in

Do use familiar tunes and write your own words

### ● Behaviour

Do make sure that parents and carers know they are responsible for their children

Do offer support to a parent/carer whose child is going through a difficult stage

Don't discuss the behaviour of their child in front of others

Do remember there is nearly always a reason for bad behaviour, eg boredom, neglect, inappropriate play, tiredness, hunger etc

Do develop positive strategies for dealing with common behaviour patterns in young children, eg biting, pushing, unwillingness to share, tantrums, dirty nappy!

Do encourage parents and carers to deal with difficult behaviour and

Don't intervene unless a child is in danger

### ● Craft

Do protect tables, floors and children if using messy materials

Do supervise at all times

Do let the children do the activity! (Provide additional materials if adults want a go.)

Don't worry too much about the end product

Do have hand-washing facilities ready

Don't allow the activity to go on too long

Do create drying space for activities needing to dry

Do be sure to put the child's name on the activity at the start

Do allow children to take them home – make more if you need a display

Do make the most of creating displays – it is a presence of the group in their absence

### ● Prayer

Do make prayers short, simple and spontaneous

Do try using a candle, bell or simple prayer song to introduce a prayer time

Do encourage different kinds of prayer, eg 'thank you', 'sorry' and 'please' prayers

Don't always insist on hands together, eyes closed

Do encourage action, rhyme and song prayers

Don't miss the opportunity to send written prayers into the home through craft activities

Do consider writing your own special prayer for the group that the children can learn and grow familiar with

### ● Involving parents and carers

Do spend time fostering good friendships with parents and carers

Do make clear to them that they are responsible for their children

Do encourage maximum participation at all times

Don't expect a parent/carer with more than one child to carry responsibility for activities

Do look out for hidden talents and leadership skills

Don't reject genuine offers of help and support

Do affirm, support and encourage parents and carers at all times.

Working with young children is hard work but we gain far more than we ever give. Be warned – shopping in your local supermarket will never be the same again. You will be gurgled at, sung to, waved at and clearly shouted at from one end of the freezers to the other. Entering the world of young children in your community will provide you with a whole new family! And together you will become part of God's family.

# Additional resources

to help and support you in your work with young children and their parents/carers.

## Recommended Children's Bibles and storybooks

*The Beginners Bible* (Zondervan)

*The Lion First Bible* (Lion Publishing)

*Lift the Flap Bible* (Candle Books)

*Me Too! Books*, Marilyn Lashbrook (Candle Books) 16 different titles with interactive stories from both the New and Old Testament

*Tiddlywinks: My Little Red Book – First Steps in Bible Reading*, Ro Willoughby (Scripture Union)

*Tiddlywinks: My Little Blue Book – First Steps in Bible Reading*, Penny Boshoff (Scripture Union)

*Action Rhyme series,* Stephanie Jeffs (Scripture Union) 4 titles:

*Come into the Ark with Noah; March Round the Walls with Joshua; Follow the Star with the Wise Men; Share out the Food with Jesus*

Bible Concertina books, Nicola Edwards and Kate Davies (Scripture Union)

*The Creation; Noah's Ark; The Christmas Baby*

The Bible Pebbles series, Tim and Jenny Wood (Scripture Union)

*Daniel in the Lion's Den; Jonah and the Big Fish; Moses in the Basket; Noah's Ark; The First Christmas; The First Easter; Jesus the Healer; Jesus the Teacher*

The Little Fish series, Gordon Stowell (Scripture Union)

Lots of titles about Jesus, other Bible people, and you and me.

Jigsaw Bible activity books 2, 3 and 4 (Scripture Union)

*Things Jesus Did, Stories Jesus Told, People Jesus Met, Baby Jesus*, Stephanie Jeffs (Bible Reading Fellowship)

## Prayer Books

*Pray and Play*: 101 Creative prayer ideas for use with under-fives, Kathy L Cannon (Scripture Union)

*The Pick a Prayer Series*, Tim and Jenny Wood, illustrated by Suzy-Jane Tanner (Scripture Union), 4 spiral-bound board titles:

*Pick-a-prayer: For Bedtime; Pick-a-prayer: For Every Day; Pick-a-prayer: For Special Days; Pick-a-prayer: To Say Thank You*

*My Little Prayer Box*, (Scripture Union)

*Hello God, it's me*, Stephanie King and Helen Mahood (Scripture Union)

*The Lion Book of First Prayers*, Sue Box (Lion Publishing)

*What Shall We Pray About?* Andy Robb (Candle)

*Prayers with the Bears* (John Hunt Publishing) 4 titles

*101 Ideas for Creative Prayer* and *New Ideas for Creative Prayer*, Judith Merrell (Scripture Union)

## Song/Rhyme Books

*Let's Sing and Shout*! ed. Maggie Barfield (Scripture Union)

*Let's All Clap Hands*! ed. Maggie Barfield (Scripture Union)

*Jump Up If You're Wearing Red* (NS/CHP)

*Feeling Good!*, Peter Churchill (NS/CHP)

*Bobby Shaftoe, clap your hands*, Sue Nicholls, (A&C Black) Includes 37 familiar and traditional tunes with simple guitar chords)

*Kidsource Books 1 and 2* (Kevin Mayhew). A general selection for children, including many suitable for under-fives.

## Other resources

*God and Me series*, exploring emotions and Christian beliefs (Scripture Union):
*Really, really scared; Really, really excited; I love you; I miss you,* Leena Lane
*What's heaven like?; What's God like?; What's in the Bible?; Can Jesus hear me?* Stephanie King

## Resources to support parents and carers

Lion Pocketbook Series, various authors (Lion Publishing) Over 15 different titles on both faith-searching issues, eg *Why Believe?; Why Pray?*, and pastoral issues, eg *Why Marry?; When a child dies*. These are inexpensive pocketbooks ideal for use with parents and carers.

*First Steps* Video for parents inquiring about infant baptism, (CPAS)

*Welcome to Baptism*, Journey of a Lifetime Video, Grayswood Studio

*Time out for Parents*, Positive Parenting Publications, First Floor, 2A South Street, Gosport PO12 1ES. A comprehensive teaching pack, covering most aspects of parenting from infancy to teenage years

*Just a minute: Biblical reflections for busy mums*, Christine Orme (Scripture Union)

Family Caring Trust
Director: Michael Quinn, 44 Rathfriland Rd, Newry, Co. Down, N Ireland BT34 1LD
*The Family Caring Trust produce an extensive range of parenting courses focusing on different age ranges of children. These have been widely used and appreciated in pre-school community groups.*

CARE for the Family P.O. Box 448
Cardiff CF15 7YY
*CARE produce a wide range of resources to support parents including a video based course called Parent Talk, books, training and special parent and child weekends.*

Courses for parents/carers who wish to explore questions and issues of faith:

*Emmaus*, National Society

*Alpha*, Holy Trinity Brompton

## Additional Leaders' Resource Material

*Bubbles for Leaders* and *Bubbles for Children* curriculum material for children (Scripture Union)

*Tiddlywinks: The Big Red and Blue Books/My Little Red and Blue Books* (Scripture Union)

*Glitter and Glue: 101 creative craft ideas for use with under-fives*, Annette Oliver (Scripture Union)

*Praise Play and Paint*, Jan Godfrey (NS/CHP)

*Under Fives Alive* and *Under Fives – Alive and Kicking*, Farley, Goddard, Jarvis, (NS/CHP)

*Bible Fun for the Very Young*, Vicki Howe (Bible Reading Fellowship)

*Bible Stuff*, Janet Gaukroger (CPAS) 5 titles in the series.

The following 2 titles are packed with ideas for encouraging parents and children to celebrate the Christian year at home:
*Feast of Faith*, Kevin and Stephanie Parkes (NS/CHP)
*The 'E' Book*, Gill Ambrose (NS/CHP)

## Background Reading

*Working with Under 6s*, Val Mullally (Scripture Union)

*Children Finding Faith*, Francis Bridger (Scripture Union/CPAS)

*Bringing Children to Faith*, Penny Frank (Scripture Union/CPAS)

*Children and the Gospel*, Ron Buckland (Scripture Union)

*The Adventure Begins*, Terry Clutterham (Scripture Union/CPAS)

*Seen and Heard*, Jackie Cray (Monarch)

*Sharing Jesus with Under Fives*, Janet Gaukroger (Crossway Books)

## Networks and Organisations supporting work with young children

Pre-school Learning Alliance
61-63 Kings Cross Rd, London WC1X9LL

Playgroup Network, PO Box 23, Whitely Bay, Tyne and Wear, NE26 3DB

Scripture Union
207-209 Queensway, Bletchley, Milton Keynes, MK2 2EB. www.scriptureunion.org.uk
For readers in other countries, please contact your national Scripture Union office for details.

The Mother's Union
24 Tufton St, London SW1P3RB

Church Pastoral Aid Society
Jackie Cray, Advisor for Families and Under-fives, Athena Drive, Tachbrook Park, WARWICK CV34 6NG

*Playleader* – an ecumenical magazine linking Christians working with Under-fives
The Editor, Diana Turner, 125 Finchfield Lane, Wolverhampton WV3 8EY

# How to plan your group programme using Tiddlywinks

*Tiddlywinks* Big Books provide resources, ideas and activities for use in any pre-school setting. Whether you are running a carer and toddler group; a playgroup or pre-school group; a nursery or nursery school; a child-minding network; a crèche or toddler club; a conventional Sunday morning group at church; a drop-in centre, a coffee morning or a pram service – or any other place or group where under-fives gather together; *Tiddlywinks* has suggestions to help you.

Here, some pre-school practitioners choose their own options for their own different types of group, using the topic 'Jesus the storyteller' on pages 68, 69, and 72.

## Brenda's choice

Almost everything! I especially like the corn pictures (good for developing hand-eye co-ordination); the story relates well to the theme; easy to memorise the words to the song, they'll know the tune and they'll enjoy doing the actions. Children can relate to all these activities and it will improve their knowledge at the same time.

*Brenda's class of twenty-seven children nearly all speak Afrikaans, with only two who are bi-lingual. She particularly liked the Pray time activity in this session: 'What a lovely way of teaching children to pray to God talking about everything!'*

## Annette's choices

*Annette runs a crèche for under-threes during the Sunday morning service at her church; she's also involved in Sunday School.*

For crèche

We've got a sandpit and we'd also do play dough: we haven't got access to a kitchen and we only use the one room. We'd make the headbands — painting is too messy with children in their best clothes! Story, rhyme, song and pray would all be 'yes' items — possibly with individuals rather than the whole group. Farm play is a good activity for this age group. We don't have any adults staying, but the children would take home their activity sheets so they'd know what we'd been doing.

For Sunday School (four to sevens)

We don't have play equipment available for this group, but we'd do both game ideas: the bean bag idea is easy and good fun. We'd make the headbands — and wear them! I'd involve the children as characters in the story and reinforce it with the song and the rhyme. The pray idea makes prayer interesting! We'd begin the activity sheet if we had time and the children would take it home to finish.

*Marinda, a nursery school teacher for four-to-five-year olds in South Africa says 'My children enjoy doing or trying out new things all the time.'*

## Marinda's choice

I'd do all of it! We do a lot of creative things – this gives us new ideas. The Play time links in with the Bible story and helps children to visualise what they're hearing about. My children love singing and movement and the prayer teaches them to be grateful for what they have.

As adults we usually just worry about the child and don't think about our own feelings: Adults too gives us all a chance to grow spiritually. And the activity page gives the parent and child the opportunity to talk about what they have learned, at home.

## Gillian's choices

For 'Tots'
*Play*: we haven't the equipment for sand play but we'd do the supermarket idea. We've not enough supervision to have free painting but we'd make bird headbands and wear them as we said the rhyme. Our group is not set up for structured games and we don't have a story (we're very chatty!) I think our adults would find we give a friendly welcome. I'd have the activity sheet available for people to choose to take one if they wanted.

For 'Playchurch'
We include themed play in our worship: sand play or supermarket shopping would work well in our space. Might do play dough too but that would probably be enough. And the bread rolls would be a 'making' activity. 'Yes', to the beanbag game and the corn pictures: that will involve the parents too as they can join in. I'd use the rhyme instead of the story and children will love the 'hands on' participative style of the prayer. We wouldn't have time for much else and remember the planting grass idea for another time. I'd use the toy farm 'extra' and remember the planting grass idea for another time.

*Pastoral assistant Gillian has been leading 'Tots' carer and toddler group for eight years, providing a safe environment for play and friendship. For half of that time she's also led 'Playchurch', a pre-school worship time for families who are unable to attend a formal service on Sunday but who can meet midweek.*

## Sue's choices

For nursery
Sand play is a good introduction to the theme. Abstract art in Making time sounds lovely – very hands on and do-able. I'd choose the game and I'd use the rhyme rather than the story – it gets the point across with lots of participation and involvement: it could be repeated lots of times. Then the song reinforces it too – good to have that change of activity. The prayer centres the session God-ward and yet keeps the children involved. Lovely extra ideas but we'd need a longer session. The activity sheet is lovely for this age group.

For reception
Sand play is a good gentle introduction to gardening and planting. Everyone's involved in the game and we'd paint corn pictures. The story is good for developing concentration and listening skills; I'd probably not use the rhyme as well, but we'd reinforce the story with the song – I like the participation here. The prayer brings God into the equation and I'd use it to round off the session. Not really enough time for any extras. The activity sheet is a good idea but a bit too much colouring-in for this age group.

*In the North of England, Sue teaches in both a pre-school nursery and reception class (first year of 'formal' education) in a church-run school.*

# God made water

Genesis 1:1–2; Psalm 104

## Play time

no limit

### Blowing bubbles

*You will need: plastic drinking straws, cut diagonally at one end; a small bowl of water mixed with baby bath liquid or detergent, placed on a table protected by old newspaper; towels. Before you play: roll sleeves up; remove extra layers of clothing; provide waterproof aprons.*

This is a great opportunity for children to observe and explore the properties of water and the way it changes when mixed with detergent. Before you hand out the straws, be sure to tell children to blow (not suck) gently to make bubbles. You might even like to ask the children to practise blowing before you give them the straws. Maintain constant supervision of the children. Encourage the children to feel free to investigate the bubbles and patterns made in the water and to talk about the experience. Prompt with questions, such as: 'Tell me about the colours of the bubbles', or 'Where are the big bubbles?' Have a towel ready to dry hands after the Play time.

### Swirling water

*You will need: a bowl of water as above; cooking oil; facilities for children to wash and dry their hands after the activity. Before you start: roll up sleeves; provide aprons; protect tables. Add a few drops of oil to the water and swirl it around.*

Introduce the children to this activity by telling them that you added cooking oil to the water. Explain to them that they can feel the water and talk to you about how it feels. Allow children to swirl around the water with a finger or their hands to make different patterns. Prompt the children to talk about the experience by saying something like: 'The water looks swirly to me – how does it look to you?' Make sure the children wash and dry their hands thoroughly after the Play time.

## Game time

10 mins

### Stepping stones

*You will need: large pieces of brown paper to be stepping stones placed at random on the carpet (to prevent slipping); recorded lively 'watery' music.*

Tell the children that when the music plays they can dance around in the 'water'. When the music stops they must sit on a stepping stone. This game need not be competitive. The children will just enjoy the idea of the game.

### Splish, splash, splosh

*You will need: a recording of 'watery' music.*

Tell the children to dance around to the music. When the music stops, tell them that you will shout either 'splish', 'splash' or 'splosh'.

•On 'splish' they should pretend to be rain and make trickling rain movements with their hands.

•On 'splash': be a raindrop that has fallen onto the ground.

•On 'splosh': lie flat on the floor like a raindrop that has fallen into all the other raindrops.

## Making time

10 mins

### Watery picture

*You will need: large pieces of paper; a glue stick for each child; blue, green, grey and black pieces from magazines, or crêpe or tissue paper (all placed in separate piles). Before you start: roll up sleeves; provide aprons; protect tables and floor. Have facilities for children to wash and dry their hands afterwards.*

Tell the children they can make a special 'watery picture'. Show them how to spread glue on a small area of their backing paper, choose a piece of paper from one of the colour piles and press on to the glue. Show how to overlap the pieces to make waves of different colours. Whilst children work, remind them how the water felt from one of the Play time activities. Can they tell you about the colours of the bubbles or the way the water looked when it had cooking oil in it?

## Story time

5-10 mins

### God makes water

*You will need: a triangle; a tambourine; bowl of water and funnels, jugs, pouring toys. Use these props during the story to make watery sounds whenever water is mentioned: ask individuals to come and help you make the noise when you indicate.*

*When you reach the song, make up your own tune and ask all the children to dance along with you – perhaps join hands and skip in a circle. Children love repetition, so do tell the story more than once or ask the children to retell parts of it.*

In the beginning of time – right at the start of the world – long before anyone remembers anything – God was there. God looked around and thought long and hard about making the heavens and the earth. He planned it all very carefully so nothing would be left out. It all needed to be perfect: just right; nothing missing.

God said, 'Well, I'm going to need all sorts of things in my heavens and earth. I'm going to have to think carefully about where I put everything.' So, God got busy. 'I know it's going to be hard work,' said God, 'but it will be worth it. It's going to be wonderful. I can hardly wait to see how it all turns out. I really feel so excited about my world!'

When God first started making the earth, he noticed that there was water everywhere.

'Mmm,' said God. 'This water is wonderful. It's going to be very useful and I will need lots of it.' He made sure that there were lots of different colours in the water: blue, green, grey, turquoise and even hints of red. 'That will make my water look even better,' God said.

God was so pleased with his heavens and earth that he sang a very happy song. The song went something like this:

'What a wonderful world,
What a wonderful place to be.
I am so happy with all I've made,
Just look at the earth and sea!'

God danced around and sang his song again.

God was so happy with his wonderful world that he sang and danced all night.

## Rhyme time

### Incy Wincy
*Children learn much through rhymes and will probably know some already. If not, try saying them a few times and gradually the children will join in.*

*Introduce the traditional rhyme 'Incy Wincy Spider'. This rhyme is great accompanied by hand actions: pretend that one of your hands is a spider climbing up, then pretend to be the rain with your other hand and 'wash' the spider 'out'. Next, pretend to be the sun and then make your spider-hand climb up again! Children may well know actions to this nursery favourite and show you if you are not sure!*

## Song time

### Earth and sea
*Before you start, remind the children of the story. Offer a variety of instruments to play whilst singing these songs, especially triangles or tambourines. Make up your own tune and sing God's song from the story. You can then add some more verses.*

I say:

'What a wonderful world,
How wonderful God must be.
He is so happy with all he's made,
Just look at the earth and sea!'

We say:

'What a wonderful world,
It's all for you and me.
We are so happy with all God's made,
Just look at the earth and sea!'

*Enjoy well-known 'watery' songs like: 'Rain, rain go away'; 'Michael row the boat ashore'; variations on the 'Mulberry bush', such as 'This is the way we wash our clothes/jump in puddles/swim in the pool…'*

## Pray time

### Water is good
*Bring in a plant to show the children. Point out the parts of the plant and talk about how the plant needs water. Can the children think why they too might need water? Tell the children you will all be talking to God and thanking him for the wonderful water he gives us. Suggest that they can close their eyes if they wish, as this can help everyone to concentrate while you say the prayer. Everyone can say 'Amen' at the end.*

Dear Father God,
Thank you for making water. We think water is great because it helps plants to grow and it is wonderful for us to drink. Please give us water every day.
Thank you,
Amen.

## Extra time

•Read *When the World Began* (Collect-a-Bible Story series, SU).

•Provide a water-play area with large bowls or trays of water, plastic funnels, bottles and cups. Or provide a well-supervised paddling pool.

•Water plants together, either indoors or out.

•Make up a rain song together, asking children to contribute to the words. Try setting the song to a familiar tune, for example, 'Michael row the boat ashore'.

## Adults too

Adults may like to consider the effects of drought or floods in some countries: perhaps they would like to spend a few minutes thinking or praying for people in these countries. A short video depicting these sorts of problems might be useful, or a few pictures demonstrating the extent of a disaster may be helpful together with a contact address, telephone number or email, should they wish to help practically. You could hand out relevant literature that provides further information for people to look at and digest after the discussion. Encourage open-ended discussion and debate. It is important to follow up these kind of discussions and to be practical in response, otherwise it can feel very frustrating. Two or three people might like to organise a fund-raising event for a suitable project. This can be a natural way of building relationships as well as helping people in need.

## Top tips

### Be safe!
•At no time must children be left unsupervised whilst playing with water.

•If any activities take place outside, carers must be advised in order to apply sun-block before their children are exposed to the sun.

Storytellers need to take part in stories whole-heartedly! The more enthusiastic you are, the more likely the children are to become involved in the story themselves. Use different facial expressions and vary your intonation. It can make such a difference. Be sure the children are comfortable and settled before you begin.

**ACTIVITY PAGE:**
The photocopiable activity page for this outline is on page 18

# 2 God's wonderful world
## God made the light, sun, moon and stars

*Genesis 1:3–5; 14–19; Psalms 84:11; 104; 148; Malachi 4:2*

## Play time

### Sky lights
*You will need: large pieces of black paper on which to print; several sponges cut into shape of stars, moon and sun; yellow, orange and grey/silver fairly thick paint; several large saucers containing paints. Before you start: roll up sleeves; provide aprons: protect tables; make sure children have facilities to wash and dry their hands afterwards.*

Show children how to make sponge prints using the sun, moon and star shapes. Point out the different shapes. Encourage children to share materials and to offer shapes to each other as this promotes social development. Allow children to play at mark making using sponges on the black paper and talk to them as they paint. Make sure they have plenty of space. They might like to use several pieces of paper, so be prepared with some extra pieces, just in case. You might like to talk to them about the shapes. Can they recognise any of the shapes? Do they know the names? Do any of them look the same? Do children know the names of the colours? This is a good opportunity to discuss with children how the sky looks at night. Once finished, place paintings in a safe place to dry. (Ensure the children's names are written at the top of the paper as children often like to take pictures home with them.)

Extend this play by:

•Allowing children to mix their own paint.
•Adding silver or gold glitter to paint.
•Using prepared card shapes of sun, moon and stars for children to glue onto black paper.
•Rolling dough and using shaped cutters of stars, moon and round sun.

## Game time

### Guess what I am?
*You will need: a board on which to place large cardboard cut-outs of sun, moon and stars.*

Tell the children that you are going to pretend to be the moon, sun or the stars using actions but no words. Can they guess which one you are pretending to be? The child who gets it right can place the matching picture on the board. Once children get the idea of the game they may wish to pretend to be the moon, sun or stars for others to guess.

## Making time

### Sun masks
*You will need: card; PVA glue, colouring pencils or crayons; gold and silver glitter pens or glue, shirring elastic or flat craft sticks. Leader will also need a craft knife or sharp scissors. Before you start: roll up sleeves; provide aprons; protect tables and have facilities for children to wash their hands afterwards.*

Cut circles of stiff paper or thin card, allowing two or three centimetres around the edge to make the sun's rays. Cut out the rays of the sun. An adult should make the two eye holes. Let the children draw on a face, colour in the rays, or add glitter to the rays. Fasten the masks with shirring elastic or tape a craft stick to the back for the child to hold.

## Story time

### God makes light
*You will need: a big box covered in silver foil containing a torch, lamp, glow-in-the-dark toy, luminous clock and the sun, moon and stars shapes from the game 'Guess what I am?'*

*As you tell the story, take out and show the shapes.*

At the beginning of time, God made the heavens and the earth. They didn't have any shape. It was very dark. It was like some kind of big, black, nothingy blob. And that is not how God wanted it to be. God had big ideas about how his world was going to look. He knew it would take lots of serious thinking and hard work. But God was ready for that.

God wanted it all to be very beautiful. But that was no good if no one could see it! So, God said, 'Let there be light.'

God made the sun to light up the day and the moon to light up the night. 'I love this,' God said. He loved the warm, golden light of the sun. He loved the cool, silver light of the moon.

'I'll make something else, just for fun,' said God. He made all the stars we can see in the sky, and lots more, too far away for us to see: big ones and little ones, all shining brightly. There were stars everywhere in the sky. Some were close together and made patterns in the sky.

God thought the light was wonderful. He

was so pleased with how it looked, God began to gather up all the light and put it in one place and then he put all the darkness in another place. God was even more pleased. 'I'm going to call all the darkness "night" and the light "day."' he said.

God was very pleased with the light because he knew we would be able to see all the wonderful things he had made. So, he sang:

'What a wonderful world,
What a wonderful place to be.
I am so happy with all I've made,
Just look at my earth and sea!'

And with that, God got up and danced around and sang his song again:

*(repeat verse above)*

Then, God sang and danced all night.

*What else have you got in your box? Look and see. Show each item and ask the children to tell you what they do.*

## Rhyme time

### Sparkling stars
*Most children will know 'Twinkle twinkle little star'. Try adding some actions, eg make tight fists then open and shut your fingers to make shining stars. Use similar actions to this variation:*

Sparkle, sparkle, tiny star.
I know just what you are.
You're a light up so high.
Like a torch in the sky.
Sparkle, sparkle, tiny star.
I know just what you are.

## Song time

### Sun, sun, sun
*Pretend to put a sun hat on and ask the children if they know what you are doing. Do the same with sun cream. Tell the children that before they sing a song they need to pretend to put their hats and sun cream on too! Sing, 'The sun has got his hat on'.*

*Learn this song to the tune of 'Three blind mice'.*

Sun, sun, sun. *(repeat)*
Rain, rain, rain. *(repeat)*
The sun is coming out again. *(repeat)*
Shine, shine, shine. *(repeat)*

*Encourage the children to accompany the song with actions. Show them how to raise their hands and spread out the fingers for the sun; then make trickling movements with their fingers for 'rain'. For the third line hide both hands and then gradually move them into view.*

## Pray time

*Bring a picture chart of things we enjoy about warm weather: paddling pools, summer clothes, holidays, flowers, fruit, ice-cream.*

*Allow children time to tell you about past holidays or ones they are about to have. This kind of discussion is valuable as it helps build relationships. Then, tell them that you are going to say a very short prayer: suggest they listen hard but keep their eyes open while you pray so they can see the light all around them.*

Dear Father God,
Thank you for making the light – it really does help us see all the beautiful things you have made. We think the moon is wonderful. We think the stars are so pretty. And the sun is really helpful to us. Thank you for the light you have made for us,
Amen.

## Extra time

•Read *The Creation* by Nicola Edwards, SU.

•Encourage children to dance like the sun, moon or stars. Provide them with long pieces of shiny, yellow, silver or orange material to wave around as they dance to represent beams of light.

•Play music that might help children to think of the sun, moon or stars.

•Provide children with a piece of paper with the words 'The sun helps the flowers grow'. Let them colour the top half blue and the bottom green. Give them a yellow circle for the sun to be stuck at the top, and then cut out or choose pictures of

flowers from gardening catalogues, to stick on the green part.

## Adults too

There are many popular theories about how the world came into being. The concept of a creator God may be challenged by some adults. Think about what you believe. Can you explain your Christian belief, if someone asks you? They won't necessarily be challenging you, just interested to hear what you have to say. It might be worth thinking or meditating on the various wonderful things in our world and making reference to the many verses in the Bible that promise the presence of a loving heavenly father who cares very much for his people and has given over the responsibility for care and maintenance of the world to people. Is it possible that such design and beauty could be thrown together without any pre-thought, as if by accident? Is it, in fact, harder to believe that the world came into being just by accident?

## Top tip

Careful planning and preparation make all the difference! Check that you have all the necessary props before you begin a story and be sure to have read through the story several times before you tell it, so that you don't have to look at every word. Telling the story, rather than reading it is very useful as you can look at the children and truly interact with them. Practise in front of a mirror to get a sense of how the children see you.

**ACTIVITY PAGE:**
The photocopiable activity page for this outline is on page 19

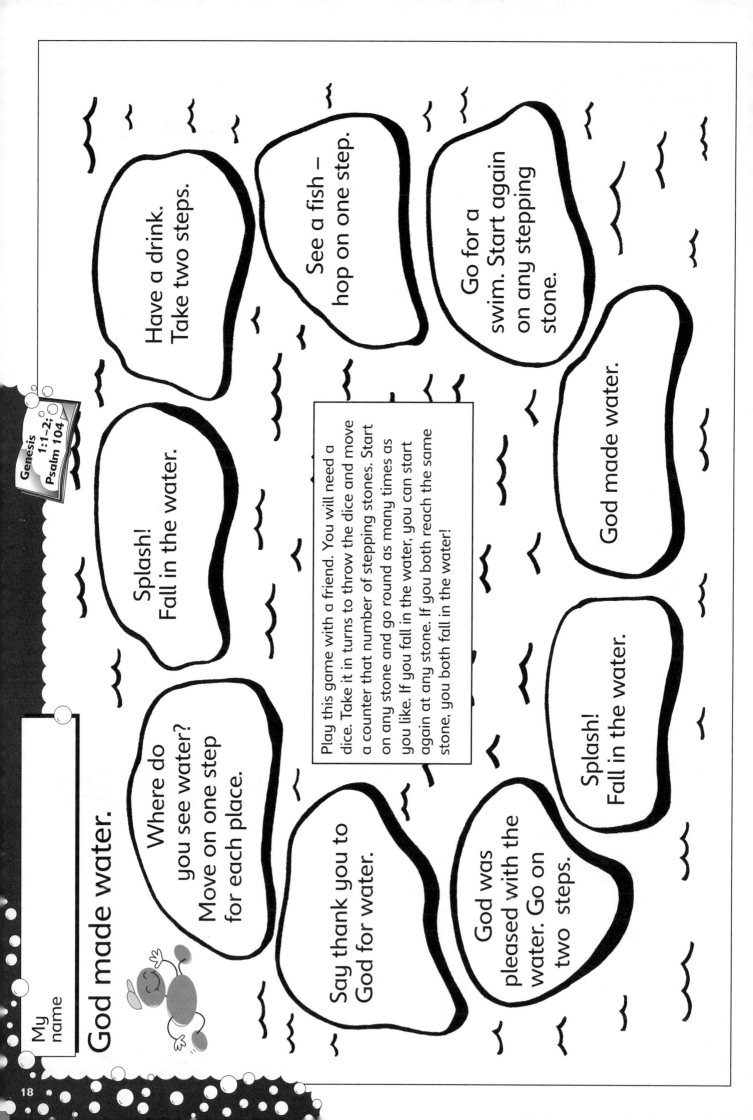

God made water.

My name

Genesis 1:1–2; Psalm 104

Where do you see water? Move on one step for each place.

Have a drink. Take two steps.

See a fish – hop on one step.

Go for a swim. Start again on any stepping stone.

Splash! Fall in the water.

God made water.

Say thank you to God for water.

God was pleased with the water. Go on two steps.

Splash! Fall in the water.

Play this game with a friend. You will need a dice. Take it in turns to throw the dice and move a counter that number of stepping stones. Start on any stone and go round as many times as you like. If you fall in the water, you can start again at any stone. If you both reach the same stone, you both fall in the water!

God made the
sun, the
moon and
the stars.

Genesis 1:3–5;
14–19; Psalms
84:1; 104: 148;
Malachi 4:2

My
name

How many stars can you see in
the sky? Colour them in. If you
have some sticky stars or glitter
pens, add more stars in the sky.

19

# God made the sky

Genesis 1:
6–8; Psalms
104; 148

*Before you start take the usual precautions: roll up sleeves, provide aprons and cover tables with PVC cloths or old newspaper.*

Let the children print cloud patterns onto each shade of paper, using a fresh piece of cotton wool to dab on each colour of paint. Show them how to dip a fresh piece of cotton wool into glue and then place it on the cover cards. Leave all the pages to dry thoroughly. Assemble the book by lining up the pages and covers, and stapling down one edge.

## Play time

### Clouds in the sky

*You will need: paints, large pieces of black or white paper, brushes, water pots.*

Prepare palettes of shades of blue, ranging from pale whitey-blue through to deep blue-purple and red-purple. Provide a range of other colours for the children to mix their own. (They may wish to paint black clouds.) Ensure children have helped each other to pull up sleeves and have aprons on ready for painting.

Use a display board to show different photographs or pictures of the sky during the day and at night. Discuss these pictures with the children.

Show the children that you have white and black paper: let them select which colour to use. When would black be a better background colour? Encourage children to experiment with the paint and to mix their own colours too. Guide them to paint clouds all over their sheet of paper. Have plenty of spare paper so they can produce more pictures if they wish.

To extend this play:

•Provide cotton wool balls for the children to dip in paint and then dip into a glue pot to stick on a thick piece of card.

•Provide an extensive range of coloured pencils (children enjoy looking at the shades) and paper for them to colour as they wish.

•Provide ready-made cards for children to decorate using any of the methods above. Then, help them write a 'Have a Happy Day' message on the front of their card. Inside help children to write a message to someone they care about. They may wish you to scribe for them, but encourage them to have a go at writing their name, even if they only manage the first letter or use a sign such as a happy face.

## Game time

### The cloud game

*You will need: a large card cloud shape for each child; a large dice; a large piece of blue fabric for all the children to sit on ('sky'); six cards with an instruction all ending with '. . . and sit on a cloud' on one side (eg, 'turn around three times and sit on a cloud') and a number (1–6) on the other. Place the cards face down on the floor with the number of the card showing.*

Explain the rules of the game. You must sit in the 'sky' until your turn. At your turn, roll the dice and count the spots. Pick up the matching number card. An adult will help to read the card. Do what the card says, then choose a cloud shape and sit on it. Continue until everyone has had a turn and the 'sky' is empty.

## Making time

### Book of the sky

*You will need: for each child, four pages of strong paper (in shades of blue, grey and black) and two stiff card covers to make into a book. (If you have a large group, you will need extra flat space for drying the pages.) Each child will also need several cotton wool balls, a paint palette with black, grey, white and pinky-red paints, glue. You will need a stapler.*

## Story time

### God makes the sky

*Introduce the story by reminding the children that they have been thinking about the sky and the clouds in the sky. Show them any cloud pictures used earlier. Ask them what they think clouds look like. What do they think they are made of? Explain to the children that during the story they are going to join in every time they hear 'God had so much to do!' repeating the phrase each time you say it. Try encouraging them to emphasise the 'so' word. Make sure your facial expressions mirror the story.*

God was working very hard when he made the world. God had so much to do! *God had so much to do!*

There were lots of things to think about. God had so much to do! *God had so much to do!*

There were lots of things to do. God had so much to do! *God had so much to do!*

Where would he put everything? God had so much to do! *God had so much to do!*

And, what they would be called? God had so much to do! *God had so much to do!*

No one had made anything before so nothing had a name. God had so much to do! *God had so much to do!*

Quite a job! God had so much to do! *God had so much to do!*

Deciding on the right names for everything was quite a job. God knew each name would be important. God had

so much to do!
*God had so much to do!*

He went through a whole list of possible names for the 'big blue bit'. In the end God decided on 'sky'. The name felt just right. God was really pleased. In fact God felt delighted with the name. God had so much to do!
*God had so much to do!*

So, now God had names for several things he had made so far: 'heavens', 'earth', 'light', 'day', 'night'. And now he had 'sky' too. What a lot of thinking to get it just right!
*God had so much to do! God had so much to do!*

*Children might like to hear the story again as they often enjoy repetition. The second time try whispering every line and encouraging the children to whisper too. Then, say it again and encourage the children to shout the repeated section. They will find this great fun!*

## Rhyme time

 5 mins

### I can see the sky
*Try saying this rhyme together and point to the sky as they say the rhyme. Repeat it several times.*

I can see the sky,
The sky so blue.
There it is,
There it is,
Way, way up high!

I can see the clouds,
The clouds so light.
There they are,
There they are,
They look so white!

### God's world
Thank you for the world you made,
All around and near and far.
Every lovely thing we see,
Shows how wonderful you are.
Clear blue sky and fluffy clouds,
Silvery moon and brightest star.
Every lovely thing we see,
Shows how wonderful you are.

## Song time

 5 mins

### White white clouds
*Introduce the singing time by talking about the wonderful sky God has made. Look out of the window (if this is possible and safe) and ask the children to comment on what they can see.*

*Start singing the song and the children will join in. Try moving your hands like clouds in the sky and moving them along when the song suggests this. Sing these words to the tune of 'Michael row the boat ashore'.*

White white clouds,
Blue, blue sky,
Moving – moving.
White white clouds,
Blue blue sky,
Up so high.

*Children might like to take it in turns to sing a solo or a few of them may enjoy singing to the rest of you. Encourage them to try this and make a point of thanking and clapping each one.*

Other songs
'I can sing a rainbow'

## Pray time

    5 mins

### Thank you for the sky
*Discuss with the children the colours of clouds; perhaps show them the picture from the Play time activity. Do they know why clouds can be grey and black sometimes? (Children can be fascinated to know a little about the way weather happens.) How does the blue sky make them feel? Does it remind them of holidays?*

*Ask the children to repeat each line of prayer after you.*

Dear Father God,
Thank you for blue sky.
Thank you for white fluffy clouds.
Thank you for little wispy clouds.
Thank you for the way clouds move along in the sky.
Thank you for all the hard work you put into making the world.
We think it's great!
Thank you!
Amen.

## Extra time

•Provide the children with a range of home-made instruments and ask them to make up a song about the sky. Give them some suggestions if they get stuck, but let them be as independent as possible.

•If the weather is suitable and you have a safe area outside, lie down on the grass and look up at the sky. (Take care to avoid looking towards the sun.)

## Adults too

Talk about the importance of names, perhaps how they chose the names of their children or what their names mean. Bring along a book of biblical names and their meanings. How important do people think Old Testament and New Testament names were? Do they think their names influenced their actions, that they were a kind of 'prophecy' as to how these people would act in their lives? Do they have names for their pets? Do they have any meaning? Do people have names for their houses or other inanimate objects? Why have they chosen them? Do any of the names they have chosen have significance?

## Top tip

When reading to young children it livens up the whole event when you get the expression and intonation just right: the whole story becomes far more engaging for the young child. It's easy to feel embarrassed when other adults are watching, especially in the parts that require exaggerated acting skills! Try to relax and concentrate on the children: they will be so engrossed that they won't want you to abandon the story and change your style!

**ACTIVITY PAGE:**
The photocopiable activity page for this outline is on page 24

# 4 God's wonderful world
# God made the land

Genesis 1: 9–10; Psalms 104; 148

## Play time

    5–10 mins

### Sorting

*You will need: a table covered with newspaper for your sorting area; fairly thick paint and a large piece of thick paper for printing. Spread out a collection of natural objects, keeping back one of each type. You could use: pebbles, leaves, twigs, cones, pieces of tree bark or flower heads. Tape or glue one of each item to a basket or plastic container.*

Show the children your nature collection and encourage them to name each of the objects. Where do they think you found them? Have they ever collected anything like them? (They will probably want to talk about their holidays.) Show the children the labelled baskets. Can they place a few items into each of the correct containers? Encourage them to feel the objects and name them as they sort them out. (Wash and dry hands afterwards.)

Once children have sorted the objects they may wish to print using a variety of the objects. Allow them to experiment with making prints.

### Land, sky and sea

*You will need: brown, blue and green play dough (sufficient amounts for all children). If you are making your own dough, use different types of flour to get different textures. Protect the working area and ensure children have rolled up sleeves.*

Explain that you are thinking about the land, sky and sea today and that they might wish to think about this as they play with the dough. Link the colours of the dough to natural features. Try introducing interesting words for the children to describe the substance of play dough: lumpy, smooth, dry, hard, soft. (It doesn't matter if the children decide to make other objects with the dough.)

Extend this activity by providing a variety of tools for the children to roll, stretch and pull the play dough.

## Game time

   5–10 mins

### Land, sea and sky game

*You will need: recorded music. Make three large flags: a brown one to represent the land, a blue one to represent the sky and a blue-green one to represent the sea. Now place these flags in three different corners of the room. If possible let them 'fly' by attaching them to a pole; if not, just attach them to a leg of a chair.*

Tell the children that the brown flag shows where the land is, the blue flag shows where the sky is and the blue-green where the sea is. Then, explain that you are going to play some music whilst they dance around. When the music stops, you will shout 'land', 'sky' or 'sea' and they have to run and stand by the correct flag. This game need not be competitive, as children will probably just enjoy the game for itself.

## Making time

   10–15 mins

### Turning Japanese

*You will need: a few pictures of a Japanese-style garden to inspire the children, shallow seed trays or plastic containers, lots of different sized stones, gravel, lots of old newspaper, play sand, aluminium foil, twigs, moss, grit, smooth pebbles, shells, small doll's house garden furniture. Encourage children to help each other roll up sleeves and put on aprons.*

Talk to the children about God making the land. Show them all the things you have brought in for them to make a small garden. The children will probably be quite excited to make their gardens, but it is worth spending a few minutes talking through the best way to do this. Don't insist on a certain design, but give general advice. For example, put a layer of sand down first. Almost one-to-one adult

help will make this a success, but try to encourage the children to be independent. They will be intrigued at making a garden without plants but be vigilant when they are handling stones and other small items to ensure the pieces go on the gardens and not in mouths, noses or ears! Ensure the children wash their hands after this activity.

## Story time

    5–7 mins

### God makes land

*You will need: an overhead projector and screen or pale wall; transparencies showing:*
*1 just black*
*2 blue/green water and flashes of white or yellow/gold*
*3 blue/green for water and sky blue for sky*
*4 black parts and 'watery' parts*

*Make these by colouring plain acetate or use coloured acetate film to make a simple collage of colours. At the appropriate time in the story show each transparency.*

*(Show 1)*
At the beginning of time – such a long, long time ago – when God was busy making the earth and the sky – he stood back one day to look at what he had made so far.

'I've been very busy,' God thought. 'Actually, I do think that it is all shaping up rather well. I know I've still got a long way to go with lots of things to make, but I do feel very happy about how it's all going.'

*(Show 2)*
With that, God danced around a bit and turned around in his mind several new ideas for his world. He had been very busy, sorting out the light and the

darkness, making sure there was morning time and night time. It was all hard work but God enjoyed it.

'I wouldn't have it any other way,' God said as he spread his hands out. His eyes were searching back and forwards over the earth and the skies. Finally, he said, 'It's going to be so fantastic!' A big smile came over his face and his eyes sparkled.

*(Show 3)*
Then, God looked closer at the water and stooped down and said, 'Water, you must be gathered up into one place under the sky'. And it happened.

*(Show 4)*
'Right,' said God, 'I will call the dry ground "land", and all the waters "sea".

'Yes,' said God, 'I like it very much. This is a tremendous beginning to my world.'

*Set out some illustrated books about the creation story and photos of dramatic scenery (old calendars are useful sources) on a display table so the children can see and chat about them with an adult.*

When the world began, Collect-a-Bible Story series, SU.

The Creation by Nicola Edwards, SU.

## Rhyme time

### How does your garden grow?
*Sing the nursery classic 'Mary, Mary quite contrary'. Look at an illustrated rhyme book. Have you got any cockle shells or bells the children could see and handle? What else might you have in a garden?*

*Emphasise the sing-song rhythm as you say:*

God made the ground, God made clay,
God made sand for me to play.
God made compost, God made peat,
God made leaf mould for worms to eat.

God made all this for me to see.
God made our world so we should say
A big 'thank you' – God, you're so good!

## Song time

### In God's hands
*Sing or teach the first verse of, 'He's got the whole world in his hands' (JU, p60).*

*Once you've sung this through a few times with the children adapt the words to suit the creation theme, eg 'He's got the dry land in his hands…' and 'He's got the big sea…'*

*You might like to provide the children with a number of different home-made instruments to play and enjoy whilst singing this song together.*

## Pray time

### God's world
**You will need:** *transparencies and projector, as for Story time. This activity will work effectively after the story, but need not follow it immediately.*

*Go through each overhead transparency again to remind the children of the story. Encourage them to retell the story. Can they remember each section? As you place each transparency on the screen encourage the children to repeat a simple phrase after you, like:*

Thank you God for the land…
Thank you God for the waters…

*At the end say 'Amen' together.*

## Extra time

• Sing 'The day I went to sea, sea, sea…'

• Sit on the floor, sing and play 'Row, row, row your boat…'

• Grow cress on damp cotton wool or in half eggshells.

• Explore different types and textures of soil: eg, have trays of compost, garden soil, play sand, builders' sand, gritty soil. Look at them and describe the differences.

• Set up a wormery and let the worms mix different colours of soil together. (Tend it carefully and visit it regularly.)

## Adults too

Discuss with adults about different lands and places you've travelled to, or would like to travel to. Bring along several books or posters showing different lands and customs. If you have a photograph album you might like to share your travelling experiences. Were there any times you felt misunderstood? How do people think refugees to our country might feel? How can their needs best be met? (Current political and social events will have relevance here: what does Christianity have to say about recent events? Have any church leaders made public statements which have led to positive or negative responses?) Try opening up a discussion about the importance of recognising other lands and cultures and the importance of shared understanding, tolerance and respect. Encourage the adults to talk about the lands they might have travelled to or where they too would like to go. What have they noticed about different customs and practices? How can Christianity have relevance in a multi-cultural society without compromising the principles applied in Christianity?

## Top tip

Try to introduce new vocabulary connected with each theme, as this will enhance the children's understanding of the subject. Allow as much discussion as possible, as this encourages children to think through their thoughts, ideas and feelings. Be sure to encourage children to listen to each other and to take turns in speaking as this encourages social development.

**ACTIVITY PAGE:**
The photocopiable activity page for this outline is on page 25

Genesis 1: 6–8; Psalms 104; 148

My name

# God made the sky.

Count how many clouds there are up in the sky. Colour them different colours.

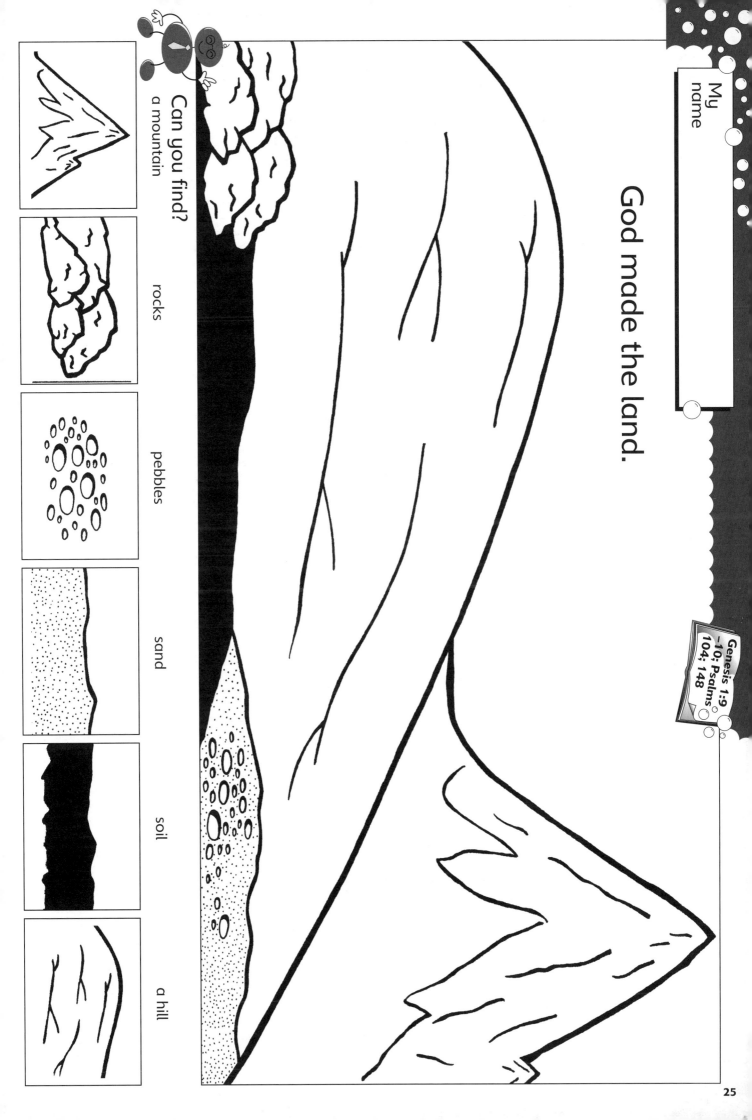

God made the land.

My name

Genesis 1:9 –10; Psalms 104; 148

Can you find?

a mountain

rocks

pebbles

sand

soil

a hill

# God made plants

Genesis 1:11–13; Psalms 104, 148

## Play time

### Leaf printing

*You will need: a variety of leaves (sufficient for each child to make a choice of at least four varieties); large thick sheets of coloured paper; thick paint using colours which reflect the leaf colours; paint*

*brushes; newspapers for covering tables. Before you start: roll up sleeves, provide aprons, cover tables. Make sure you have facilities nearby for hand washing and drying. Encourage children to help each other roll up sleeves and put on aprons. It is important that they learn to help and care for one another.*

Depending on your venue and the amount of adults involved with the group, you could go out and collect the leaves for this activity together. Show and talk about the different leaves you have collected. Can the children name any of the trees from which the leaves come? Can the children name the colours of the leaves? Encourage the children to apply thick paint to one side of a leaf and press firmly onto a sheet of paper. Children might like to create a pattern with the leaves. Once a sheet is complete ask the children to place them on a drying rack or on a separate table to dry. Ensure their names are written at the top or on the back of each piece of paper. If children are unable to write their name, then encourage them to draw a symbol at the top of the paper, perhaps a smiley face or a flower. The children will have their own ideas. Encourage children to be as independent as possible when washing their hands, although you will always need to supervise this part of the activity.

To extend this play you could cut out the prints and make a tree montage, adding bark rubbings for the trunk and main branches.

## Game time

### Garden game

*You will need: thick cardboard, thick marker pens, counters and dice. Up to four children can play at once, with an adult to supervise and guide. You may need to make more boards or repeat the activity several times so everyone can play.*

Devise a large, simple playing board. Draw a path around the outside of a square piece of cardboard. Divide the path into about ten spaces and write a number on each space. Write a short message on spaces 3, 6 and 8, something like 'Water your plants. Move on 2 spaces.'

Either show the children a variety of plants and/or bring in a few very unusual looking plants. Once you have discussed what they look like, tell the children that they are going to play the board game. You will need to read the messages on the board for them.

## Making time

### Miniature gardens

*You will need: small seed trays or plastic containers, lots of old newspaper; potting compost, aluminium foil, twigs, evergreen leaves and moss, grit, stones and pebbles, small plant cuttings, dried flowers, chairs*

or tables from small world toys. (Ensure that all plant material is non-toxic and safe for children to handle.) Extra adult help would be very useful. Encourage children to help each other roll up sleeves and put on aprons.

Talk to the children about today's theme and show them all the things you have brought in for them to make a small garden. The children will probably be quite excited and eager to make their garden, but spend a few minutes talking through the best way to work. For example, put the compost in first; handle the plants gently. Almost one-to-one adult help will make this activity a success, but try to encourage the children to explore their own ideas and generate their own designs. Ensure that the children wash their hands thoroughly after this activity.

To extend this play, you could dampen the compost and sprinkle on some grass or cress seeds. Over the next few days, the garden will grow! Children will enjoy watching this if you have a daily session or they can take their own gardens home, water them lightly and watch what happens.

## Story time

### God makes plants

*You will need: some plants or large pictures of plants.*

*Aim to show something of the range and variety of plant life on earth. Show the plants to the children, then display them on a low table while you tell the story.*

When God was making the world, he had all sorts of good ideas about how to use colours. He was very keen to use all the colours he could possibly think of – to show just how much he enjoys giving us everything! God started to go through all the colours, from white all the way through greens and purples to a deep, deep shade of black.

'Mmm,' said God, 'I must use up all my colours. I don't want any left over. I'll start with the big trees. They will use up lots of colours, especially if I make sure flowers grow on some of them.' So, God made trees. When God had finished that bit, he was pleased to have used up lots of brown, especially on the bark of trees, and green on their leaves. But God still had lots of greens left over. What should he do with them?

'I know,' said God, as a terrific idea came to him. 'Plants. I need plants. That will use up more shades of green.' So God made plants – of all shapes and sizes. And even more shades of green! Just for fun! Then, some of the plants needed flowers on them. 'Great,' said God, 'I can invent more bright colours for flowers. Oh what fun! This is marvellous!' So God made flowers in pinks and reds and purples, blues and greys and yellows. Even black! Even green! Just then a happy thought came to him.

'Why not have some trees and plants which have bits on them to be eaten?' said God. 'Good! Another chance to use up my bright colours. I'll make oranges, pineapples, pears, apples. Yes, that is what I'll do.' So God made fruit and vegetables and all sorts of plants to eat.

Soon, God had used up all the colours he could think of (and don't forget he had even made shades of all the colours too).

God was very pleased with how his world was shaping up. He danced around the trees and flowers looking at each one he had made. And they all looked great.

## Rhyme time

### All God's plants
*This sing-songy rhyme can be combined with Rhyme time in the previous section (page 23)*

God made the land, God made the earth,
God made the soil to give plants birth.
God made flowers, God made weeds.
God made them grow from tiny seeds.

God made all this for me to see.
God made our world so we should say
A big 'thank you' – God, you're so good!

### Other rhymes
*'Swing me low, swing me high'* (traditional)
*'Growing seeds', 'Small seeds', 'A seed is planted',* LSS, pp 9–10.
*'God made', 'Up popped the seeds', 'God shows his care', 'Sow the seeds', 'Seeds and soil', 'How things grow'* all in LACH.

## Song time

### All God's plants
*Sing to the tune of 'We plough the fields and scatter.'*

We scatter seeds and plant the bulbs,
In all the earth God made.
We know it's fed and watered
By God's helpful hand.
He sends everything plants need;
The sun, the warmth, the rain.
Our God is so wonderful
For all the plants he made.

All good things around us,
Are sent by God himself,
So let's thank God,
Yes, let's thank God,
For everything is good.

### Other songs
'I can sing a rainbow'
'Ring-a-ring-a-roses' (traditional)

## Pray time

### My favourite things
*Ask the children to think of their favourite plant or flower, and colour before you start. Have a range of different real items or pictures to show them and prompt their ideas.*

Pray in turn round the circle. Don't close eyes to pray: instead, use your eyes to look at the examples. When it is their turn to say 'Thank you God for … (favourite plant and colour)' they name their own favourites. Demonstrate what you mean, eg, 'Thank you God for lavender. I like the way it smells and I like the colour blue.' Then show the children some lavender and something blue. Help them do the same with their favourites.

## Extra time

•Paint flowers on paper – real or imaginary ones.

•Music and movement: dance like fluttering leaves, grow like a tiny seed, stand tall and stately like a tree.

•Children can pretend to be a plant and

you will try and guess which one they are! You might like to demonstrate the game yourself first, eg a cactus plant is all spiky, so you could spread your fingers out to look all spiky.

•Make paper tissue flowers. String them together to make a Hawaiian lei garland.

•Make a flower, with a chenille wire stem and crêpe paper petals, for someone they care about. Children may like to make two flowers, one to keep and one to give away.

## Adults too

Adults might like to discuss the medicinal properties of plants and herbs. What traditional methods do they know? Remember that many common remedies are derived from plants. You might like to research this area first yourself. Go to the library or look it up on the internet. You could discuss this from the environmental angle: many of our medicines come from tropical plants and yet tropical forests are being destroyed faster than new species can be discovered. Also, there are several religions which base some of their philosophies on herbal remedies and other practices and 'spiritual' beliefs. How can you tell which is acceptable and compatible with Christian belief? There are several Christian books on the market which deal effectively with this subject: do ask at your local Christian book shop.

## Top tip

Imagination and creativity are gifts from God. When working with children don't always feel you have to stick rigidly to what is planned. You will begin to get to know the children well and be able to decide what might work best for them. So, you might like to include some ideas of your own and, as long as the children are safe, have a go!

**ACTIVITY PAGE:**
The photocopiable activity page for this outline is on page 30

# God made fish

Genesis 1: 20-23

## Play time

### Role play

*You will need: lots of pieces of long, silky fabric in shiny green, blue and yellow. Each child will need at least three pieces; recorded music which represents fishes swimming in water (something that sounds smooth and 'watery'); a large piece of cardboard cut out into the shape of a fish tank! It must be large enough for the children to pretend to be swimming around behind it. The frame can stand up against two chairs.*

Show the children the different coloured pieces of cloth. Say they can choose several pieces and pretend to be fishes swimming around in the sea or the tank. Make sure there is sufficient space so that the children don't bump into each other. Do join in with the Play time by pretending to be a fish yourself! Don't take over their play but sensitively join in: children enjoy the presence of an adult who is prepared to have fun. This will encourage them to play creatively and imaginatively. Put the music on and allow the children to play, dance and move creatively.

*Be safe!* Be sure that the pieces of material are not so long as to trip the children up, but of a sufficient length to create a good effect.

### Options:
•Provide large drawings of reeds and place them around the room to create an underwater atmosphere.
•Hang long green shapes from the ceiling to create an underwater atmosphere.
•Play a game around the theme of under the water. When the music stops they need to go to a certain place (behind a stone, into the wreck – these can be furniture or parts of the room).

## Game time

### Magnetic fishing

*You will need: a magnetic fishing game with rods, or make your own fishing game by cutting out fish shapes (children could colour them in first) then attaching paper clips to each one. Erect a piece of thick cardboard which will form the frame of the 'pond'. Make fishing rods by tying short pieces of string to pencils. Attach a small magnet to the end of the string.*

Ensure that there is a rod for each child. If you have more than four children you may need to supply two separate games, or repeat the game several times. Encourage the children to take turns. Keep the game non-competitive and be sporting and throw your fish back! Count how many fish there are in the pond, how many you catch, etc. Try to stimulate conversation about fishes and their different colours and sizes.

*Be safe!* Be sure that children do not swallow or choke on small items such as the magnets and clips for this activity.

## Making time

### Fish in a bowl

*You will need: different sized fishes cut out of card; a goldfish-bowl shape with the centre cut out made of strong card; cellophane or food wrap; colouring pencils; string; pencils or craft sticks; sticky tape.*

Provide the children with at least two fishes each and ask them to colour them in as they wish. Attach a piece of string to the top of each fish and then to a stick or pencil.

Give the children the cut-out shape of a goldfish bowl and ask them to colour the outline of it as they wish. Once they have finished colouring attach cellophane to the sides of the goldfish bowl to create the illusion of glass. Now help the children move their fish behind the goldfish bowl in a swimming motion.

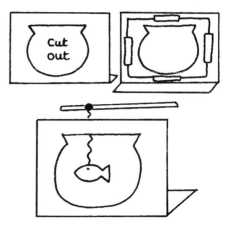

## Story time

### God makes fish

*You will need: a selection of different coloured and sized fish puppets made out of old socks (see diagram). Glue or stitch on buttons or pieces of brightly coloured felt for eyes. A puppet theatre is a good investment for work with young children: buy one, or cajole a DIY enthusiast to make you one. If you don't have a theatre, a table to hide your hand behind will be sufficient.*

*As you tell the story, bring out the appropriate fish. Try to make the fish look as though it is talking or moving around in the water. Children adore puppets and are likely to concentrate well when a story is accompanied by lively, animated puppets. You might like to retell this simple story again or the children might like to retell it for you! They would be pleased to use the puppets themselves: be sure that everyone has a go at using the puppets!*

*By now, God is about half way through making his world. If you are using all the 'God's wonderful world' themes, remind the children of what God has made so far. If you are using only this outline, explain that God made the world and everything in it and today's story is about one of the things he made.*

'Well, this world is looking good,' God said. 'I'm so pleased with all I have made so far. Now I must think about what I need next.' God looked around for a while and then stopped suddenly and said very loudly, 'Fishes! I need fishes. They are just what I need.'

So, God started to make tiny fish, big fish, odd-looking fish, beautiful fish, shiny ones, dull-coloured ones, ones with spots, ones without spots, fish with big eyes and fish with small eyes. God made so many different types of fish.

'Just what I need,' said God. God was even more pleased now and danced with joy to see all that he had made. Then, God decided to have another look at each one he had made.

The big fish.
'Just what I need,' said God.

The small fish.
'Just what I need,' said God.

The shiny fish.
'Just what I need,' said God.

The dull-coloured fish.
'Just what I need,' said God.

Each one was special. God thought they were great!
And God said, 'What a good day's work!'

## Rhyme time

**Wish for a fish!**
*Start by speaking softly and quietly and then gradually getting louder and quicker!*

*Start by whispering 'fish…'*

Fish…fish…fish…fish…fish.
*(A little louder…)*
Fish…fish…fish…fish…fish.
*(Much louder…)*
I wish for a fish…

I wish for a fish,
Splish, splish, splish,
I wish for a fish.
Wishy, washy, splishy, sploshy,

Fishy, fishy fish!

I wish for a fish,
Splash, splash, splash,
Splish, splash, splish,
I wish for a fish.
Wishy, washy, splishy, sploshy
Fishy, fishy fish!

I wish for a fish,
Splosh, splosh, splosh,
Splish, splash, splosh,
I wish for a fish.
Wishy, washy, splishy, sploshy
Fishy, fishy fish!

I wish for a fish!

## Song time

10 mins

**Fishy fun**
*Adapt the words of 'Five little ducks' to:*

Five little fish went swimming one day,
Out in the seas and far away.
Mother Fish said, 'Bubble, blubble, blome,'
And four little fish came swimming home.

*Improvise actions to go with the song: place your hands together and wiggle like a fish swimming. Move your hands far away and back again!*

## Pray time

10 mins

**God made fish**
*You will need: a simple home-made book of four pages for each child; each page showing a picture of a fish. These could be from magazines, your own drawings or computer clipart. Write on the front of the book 'God made fish'. Children can write their name in a space provided.*

*Talk to the children about the books you have made for them, say that you will say a short prayer and they can look at the fish as you pray.*

Dear Father God,
Thank you for making such brilliant fish. We think the big ones are great. We like the small ones too. Thank you for making brightly coloured and shiny fish. They look really good. Thank you,       Amen.

## Extra time

•Make a group collage: draw a huge fish and make scales by overlapping handprints or cut-out hand-shapes.

•Talk with children about fish and chips and how they are cooked.

•Provide children with large pieces of paper and paint for mixing their own colours.

•Is there an aquarium nearby that you could visit as a group day out?

## Adults too

Try opening a discussion about environmental issues particularly concerning the livelihood of our waters and water life, for example: tar, oil and the effects on creatures' habitats. What can be done? Which organisations help in these situations? Acquire a range of good literature before this event. Be sure to have sufficient copies for all adults. Try reading parts of this together and sharing experiences of environmental issues that have, perhaps, affected their lives. For example, the increase in the number of asthma sufferers.

Look out in your local press for events such as pond-dipping days, country park open days or even visits to water treatment works! Advertise these on your notice board.

## Top tips

Constant supervision of young children is essential. If adult carers do not remain with their children, be sure to have enough helpers for when the children need to go to the toilet.

Train young new volunteers. Try to make sure you have time to explain how you plan and prepare materials for the children, as well as how to set them up. Encourage all helpers to interact sensitively with children and not to talk 'down' to them.

**ACTIVITY PAGE:**
The photocopiable activity page for this outline is on page 31

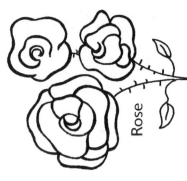
Rose

Sequoia

Genesis 1:11
–13; Psalms
104, 148

God thought of all sorts and sizes of plants. Draw your own plant here, any size, colour and shape you like!

My name

# God made plants.

Grass

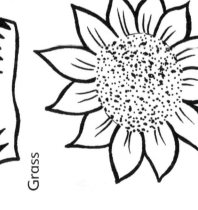
Sunflower

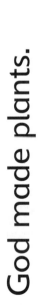

# God made fish.

Look at the fish.
Can you match the
fish to their black
shapes? Point to the
pairs.
Do you know what
these fish are called?
Ask a grown-up to
help you find the
answers.

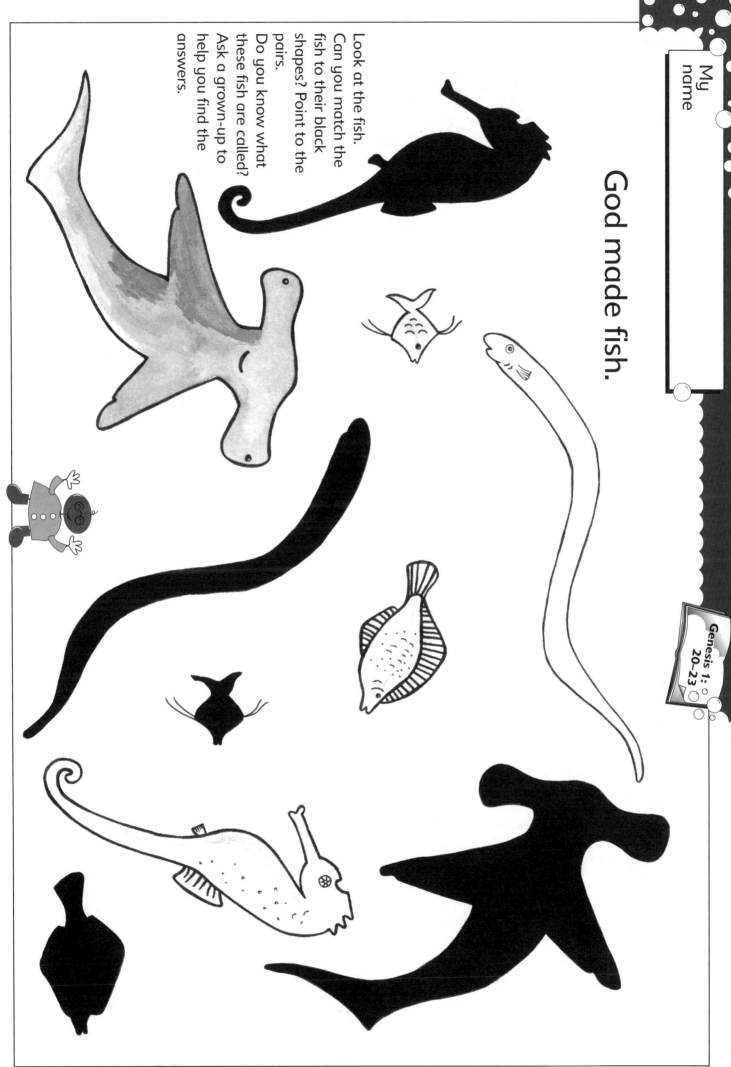

Genesis 1:
20–23

hammerhead shark, eel, flounder, seahorse, angel fish.

# God made birds

Genesis 1: 20–23

## Play time

  no limit

### Go birding

*You will need: a collection of books, magazines and pictures showing common and exotic birds. Relevant books could be borrowed from the local library. Display posters on the walls or on a board showing different species of birds. Set out an area with rugs, comfortable chairs or beanbags.*

Allow the children to browse through the books and magazines and, if appropriate, talk to them about their favourite birds. Children often enjoy the relaxation of just talking in a chatty way to adults when they are looking at books – this can provide adults with an opportunity to get to know the children in their care.

### Puppet birds

(enlarge)

*You will need: pieces of thick card, a bird template, safe scissors, colouring pencils. Before you start, roll up sleeves; provide aprons; protect tables. Children will need to be able to wash and dry their hands afterwards.*

Either cut out the bird shapes ready for the children to use, or provide templates for them to do so themselves. An adult will need to make two holes for the child's fingers to go through in order to make the bird's legs. Let the children colour in the birds and then play with their puppets.

## Game time

   10 mins

### Bird snap

*You will need: snap cards made from some wrapping paper depicting birds. Cut out the individual creatures to make the cards. Mount each one on a piece of stiff card so you have several of each design. Mix the cards up. Use the cards to play several games. Show the children how to play snap if they are not sure. Divide the pack of cards equally between all players. Four children playing at one time is a comfortable limit.*

The cards can also be used to play 'pairs': spread all the cards out face down on the table. Each player takes it in turn to turn over two cards; if the cards match, it forms a pair. If the cards do not match, they are turned face down again. Use the names of the birds frequently as you play to help the children understand that they are all birds yet different types.

## Making time

  10-15 mins

### Hungry bird

*You will need: a paper plate for each child, tissue, scraps of coloured paper.*

*Before you start: make sure the children have their sleeves rolled up and are wearing protective aprons. Cover the tables. The children will need to be able to wash and dry their hands afterwards.*

Fold a paper plate in half then unfold it. Glue a paper beak into the fold. Cut out small triangles to make feathers. Glue them on to make feathers. Draw on eyes. Cut out long strips of tissue. Stick them on the back of the bird for a tail. Spread out the tail to form feathers. The hungry bird will rock and peck.

## Story time

   7-10 mins

### God makes birds

*You will need: enough 'craft' feathers for each child to hold one as the story progresses.*

*Remind the children of the beginning of the creation story, how God began to make the earth. Say that now we are going to hear what God made next!*

In the morning, a long time ago – at the beginning of the world – God was looking into the sky he had made. God was thinking how blue the sky looked.

'Such a good choice of blue,' God said. 'I think it looks great.' Then, he began to wonder whether something was missing. 'Mmmm,' he said to himself. 'Certainly needs something up there in the sky. I must give this some thought.' And God thought for some time about it. He knew he had the moon, the sun and the stars – but he was sure something was missing.

'There must be something missing,' he said quietly. Whilst he was thinking, a leaf floated down to earth.

'That's it!' said God. 'I need something to fly around – to float – to move – to glide. It will all look so much more interesting that way.' So God set about making birds. They were all different colours and sizes. He gave them wings and feathers so that they could fly all over his sky. He made lots of different types so that they would look wonderful flying around the blue sky. He made bright peacocks and shiny starlings and glossy bower birds. He made speckled owls and tiny hummingbirds and amazing albatrosses! *(Add your own choices here to interest the children, particularly birds they will have seen locally.*) And he made tall ostriches and rounded kiwis to walk on the land, and penguins to swim in the sea.

'Just the thing,' God said. 'Beautiful birds of all different sizes and colours. I love them. They are all so very, very special.' When he had finished making all the birds he needed, God looked back up into the sky and a big smile came over his face. He looked around at the birds flying and walking and perching and hopping – and even swimming!

'Just great,' he said, as he watched them. 'Just great!' said God.

Birds that flutter right by,
Birds that fly with wings on high –
That's how they fly by!

## My wings!
*Use the paper birds again or pretend to be a bird yourself as you fly around and sing, to the tune of 'London's Burning':*

See my wings now,
See my wings now,
Spread them right out,
Spread them right out,
Watch me fly!
Watch me fly!
Feathers flapping,
Feathers flapping.

## Extra time

•Talk to children about bird watching.

•Discuss how birds have different beaks according to the food they eat.

•Talk about nests and how they are made. Try to get a good picture of a nest. Discuss why we must not disturb nests.

•Arrange a visit to a bird hide and watch birds.

•Make pretend binoculars by taping two cardboard tubes together.

•Set up a bird table or nesting boxes where the children can see them. Feeding the birds can become a regular feature of your group.

## Rhyme time

### Peck, peck, peck
*Use your thumbs and index fingers to make a pecking action for each hand. You could play this as a group game, using the same method as 'Oranges and lemons': 'catch' one of the birds at the last 'peck'.*

'I need some food,'
Said the hungry little bird,
'I haven't eaten
For a day or two now.
When will I get some
Juicy worms to eat?'
When will I get some
Tasty worms to eat?'

'Here comes my food,
Oh peck, peck, peck!
Here comes my food,
Oh peck, peck, peck!'

*Play the traditional finger rhyme game 'Two little dicky birds'.*

## Pray time

### All God's birds
*Help the children to pretend that their hands are birds. Show them how to do this, either by hooking your thumbs together or just flapping your hands around together – both are effective. Ask the children to flap their hands like birds as you say this prayer.*

Dear Father God,
We thank you for all the birds you have made.
We like looking up into the sky and seeing them fly around.
We like seeing them hopping around on the ground.
We like seeing them in the trees.
We think you are marvellous for the way you have made them.
Thank you for all your birds,
Amen.

## Adults too

Matthew 6:26–30 talks about birds demonstrating our value to God. Discuss how good it is that God cares for us and will provide for us if we trust him. Perhaps share examples of how God has met your needs: these can be physical, emotional, social or spiritual. Offer to pray for anyone who would like a need met. You could do this openly or as part of your private prayer time: gauge which is most appropriate to the situation and person concerned. Explain how simple it is to speak to God, rather like speaking to a close friend. 'Thous' and 'shalts' are really not for everyday language and God understands our modern day speech! If you pray with or for people aloud, do remember not to slip into that sort of language yourself! Encourage people to come back and tell of how God has answered their prayers.

## Song time

### Birds that fly
*You will need: a sheet of thin A4 paper folded as shown. Hold it firmly along the original fold and flap it up and down to make a simple and surprisingly effective bird.*
*The children can take their birds flying around the room! Sing to the tune of 'Pop goes the weasel'.*

Birds that fly with wings on high,

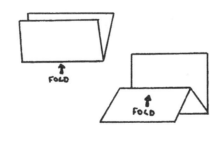

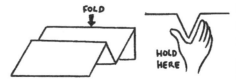

## Top tip

Hand gesture during a story can be very effective and capture the interest of children. Try flapping your hands like birds' wings as you tell the story. The children might like to join in too. You will probably have to show them how to move their hand like birds – this will be a good investment of time as it will encourage them to join in and will keep their interest.

**ACTIVITY PAGE:**
The photocopiable activity page for this outline is on page 36

# God made big animals

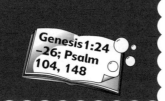

Genesis 1:24 –26; Psalm 104, 148

## Play time

no limit

### Animals

*You will need: a variety of plastic farm and zoo animals (big animals only); a variety of soft animal toys (big animals only); posters of different big animals placed on a board; green cloth placed on tables to act as grass; bean bags to create a quiet area; factual books showing different kinds of big animals.*

Share with the children times when you have seen big animals, perhaps when you were on holiday, at the zoo or on a farm. Talk to the children about their experiences of seeing big animals and encourage the children to describe them. What did they look like? What did they eat? How were they looked after? Show the children the toy farm animals you have brought in and see if they know any of their names. Children enjoy looking at factual animal books, particularly if the photographs show detail, for example, their teeth or their fur. Show them the posters and encourage them to talk about how the animal's coat might feel. Suggest vocabulary like soft, spiky, hard, smooth, etc. Can they think of how the animal might 'talk' to other animals? Do they know the noises they make?

Be sure that you have enough animal toys for all the children to play with and encourage children to share. Arrange them on tables or a mat on the floor. If possible, arrange furniture for a quiet area where the children can browse through the factual books on animals.

Allow the children to play freely with the big animal toys. You might find that some may wish to look at the books and then play with the toy animals.

*Be safe!* Some plastic animal toys are very small. Constant supervision is always required.

## Game time

10 mins each

### Lotto animals

*You will need: a commercial animal lotto game or one you have made, using card and two sets of matching square-shaped pictures of big animals. Cut out a large piece of card and glue on one set of animal pictures, in a grid pattern. Cut out the smaller individual cards and glue on the matching animal pictures.*

To play, show the children how they can place their smaller cards against the picture on the larger card. Shuffle up the cards. Give each child a large card and let them take it in turns to match up the individual animal pictures.

## Making time

15 mins

### Smile at the crocodile!

*You will need: card (green if possible), paper fasteners, colouring pencils, safe scissors. Make several crocodile templates from the diagram. Enlarge to create different sizes. Before you start roll up sleeves, protect the children and the working area. The children will need to be able to wash and dry their hands after this activity.*

Help the children draw round the crocodile. Some will need support drawing round a template. Help the children cut out the two pieces. Next, they can colour their crocodile. An adult will need to make the appropriate holes and place the fastener in the correct place.

Have several small groups each with an adult, or repeat the activity so everyone has a turn.

*Be safe!* Ensure children are careful with the paper fasteners to avoid injury.

## Story time

10 mins

### God makes big animals

*You will need: your own animal puppets made from paper bags, socks or pieces of felt glued or sewn together. Children enjoy puppets and will be delighted with something that looks vaguely like the real thing! Prepare puppets or pictures of some of the animals mentioned to show while telling the story.*

God was enjoying making his world. One day he looked all round the things he had made. God smiled.

'It's looking great!' he said, 'Lots of different colours and shapes. It really is going so well.'

God watched the stars for a while and thought how well they twinkled. He looked at the moon and was so pleased with the light it gave. Then, he stroked the petals of a flower. He was pleased with how soft it felt.

Just at that moment, God had a wonderful thought, a bigger thought, a fantastic thought.

'Animals!' he said out loud. 'Oh, wouldn't it be wonderful to have animals in my world? What a difference they would make. They could move around my world. There would be plenty for them to eat and they would look so good. Yes, I must have animals – really big animals.'

'I could make big animals with long fur and short fur. I could have ones that look stripy and fierce. I could even have some that look gentle and wise. Oh… and I could have some animals that look so bold, strong and fearless! Of course, not forgetting that I will need some of my big animals to be able to move like the wind, fast and furious. Then again, I will need some to move slowly and silently. I could even have some enormous animals to swim in my sea. Lots and lots of animals! The more the better! It really will be so good.'

Straight away, God set about making big animals. He made so many because he had so many ideas for how big animals could look and live in his world! Here are the names of a few God made: lion, tiger, bear – zebra, hippopotamus, elephant – walrus, cow, rhinoceros.

'They look grand!' God said in a loud voice. 'The big animals are just what I needed.'

And God was so pleased with them all.

How many more big animals can you think of?

*Let the children play with the puppets and/or make their own from paper bags or large envelopes.*

## Rhyme time

### We're going on a bear hunt

*Children very quickly get the idea of going on a bear hunt and you may find this game becomes a group favourite! A leader chants each line, using plenty of expression and actions; everyone repeats the line as you move round the room on your hunting trip. Beat out a rhythm, by tapping thighs or clapping.*

*The refrain goes as follows:*

> We're going on a bear hunt.
> We're going to catch a big one.
> I'm not scared!
> What a beautiful day!

Uh-oh… *(worried)*… grass.
Long, wavy grass.
Can't go under it,
Can't go round it,
We'll have to go through it.
Swish, swish, swish. *(Push through!)*

> *Refrain*

Uh-oh…*(worried)… mud*
Thick, squelchy mud.
Can't go…
  *(Squelch your feet through the mud!)*

> *Refrain*

Uh-oh,..*(worried)*… a river.
A whirly, swirly river. *(Swim across!)*

> *Refrain*

Uh-oh…*(worried)*… A forest.
A thick, tall forest. *(Stumble on!)*

> *Refrain*

Uh-oh…*(worried)*… A cave.
A deep, dark cave.
  *(Speak very slowly and deliberately.)*
Two big, staring eyes.
  *(Blink and point at your eyes.)*
One cold, wet nose.
  *(Twitch your nose and point to it.)*
Four big, furry paws.
  *(Place your hands in front of you.)*
IT'S A BEAR!
  *(Hold your hands up in mock-horror.)*
Quick! Home!

*(Reverse all the actions as quickly as possible to create tension!)*

Out of the cave, through the forest, stumble, trip, stumble, trip, across the river, splash, splash, splash, through the mud, squelch, squelch, through the grass, swish, swish, swish – phew! We're home!

## Song time

### All the animals

*Sing this new song to the tune of 'I can sing a rainbow'. Add more verses of your own, bringing in the names of the animals you are looking at today or which the children mention.*

All the animals God has made,
Lions and tigers and bears,
I can sing about them,
Sing about them,
Sing about them all.

## Pray time

### We love animals!

*You will need: access to video equipment, to play the children a short clip from a wildlife documentary. (Make sure you've checked the content first!) Or a few large colourful posters or photos of animals.*

*Discuss with the children the animals they have seen. As you pray, ask the children to join in every time you say 'Thank you God.'*

Dear Father God,
We like the animals you have made,
*Thank you God.*
We like the giraffes.
*Thank you God.*

We like the elephants.
*Thank you God…*
*(Continue as appropriate.)*

Amen.

## Extra time

• Make a zebra mask using a paper plate.

• Play music from *The Carnival of the Animals* (Saint-Saens) in the background.

• Sing and say all the songs and rhymes the children know about animals.

• Read the *Animal Tales* series by H Henning and G Chapman, SU

## Adults too

Adults often enjoy discussing conservation issues as there is so much to be debated. Carry out some research yourself before the session and see what you can find out about different kinds of zoos and their purposes and philosophy. Many zoos now have a mission statement and will be happy for you to have a copy. You can then guide the discussion into thinking about creation issues. Go through each of the stages you have taught the children so far. Discuss how God made the earth and how he provides food for all his animals, the food chain and how it operates. What happens when environmental issues have become a problem to animal life? How does this affect the food chain? Adults may wish to discuss other conservation issues.

## Top tip

Preparation is the key to a successful story time session. Be sure to have read over the story and, if possible, memorise it. Then, make sure you have all the props you need ready. Try rehearsing the story the night before and experiment with using different voices and facial expressions. Watching yourself in a mirror is quite revealing – you can soon tell if you are boring!

**ACTIVITY PAGE:**
The photocopiable activity page for this outline is on page 37

The page can be used to make a mask: this will be easier and quicker if you can copy the page directly on to card.

God made birds.

My name

Here are some flying birds.
Colour and cut them out.
Fit them together to make
a flock of birds flying along.
Copy the shape to make
more birds.

cut
away

cut
away

Genesis 1:24
–26; Psalms
104; 148

# God made big animals.

Make a lion mask.

# God made little animals

Genesis 1:24 -26; Psalms 104; 148

## Play time

no limit

### Play with little animals

*You will need: fur fabric; shiny fabric; soft fabrics; home-made animal masks or ears on headbands; 'furry' gloves and hats; posters and pictures of small animals, insects, etc; toy farm and zoo animals, and buildings if available; plastic mini-beasts; factual books about animals.*

Have some background music playing during your free play session: you may be able to find compilations of animal-themed songs and music. Gather the children together and show them the factual books and pictures of different kinds of small animals. Some show life-sized illustrations or photos – these are very popular with young children. They might wish to tell you about the small animals they have seen. Encourage this kind of discussion. If you can, think of a real-life tale about a small animal. For example, you might have had a fox or a hedgehog that used to visit your house every evening. Tell the children how you first noticed it, what the animal looked like and if it made any noise. Or you might be able to talk about your own small pet.

Use the fabrics and masks to dress up as small animals: move around the room and let each other guess which animal you are pretending to be. Allow the children free play and encourage them to play at being different small animals. Be careful that the pieces of fabric do not trip the children up.

### Mini-beasts

Improvise a game where you pretend to be small creatures. Follow-the-leader, like ants, trying to walk exactly on the same route. Be busy bees and buzz your way round the room and back to your 'home'. Crawl like a caterpillar, lie very stiff and still in a cocoon, emerge and fly like a butterfly. Slide along like a slug and crawl sideways like a crab. What else could you be?

## Game time

7-10 mins

### Jigsaw puzzles

*You will need: jigsaw puzzles of different kinds of small animals made by pasting colourful pictures onto thick card. Cut them into approximately four pieces.*

Allow the children to play with the jigsaw puzzles and encourage them to share.

### Catch the animals

*You will need: some hoopla rings made from circles of stiff card, plastic animal models, play dough or modelling clay.*

Stand several plastic animal models on a low table, holding them to the surface with some play dough or modelling clay. Show the children how to take it in turns to throw the rings and try to 'catch' an animal. Agree a distance to stand, away from the table and gently guide the children to stand back when they throw.

### Bug hunt

Hide lots of model mini-beasts around the room and go on a hunt to search them all out. When you spot one, move towards it quietly and slowly so you can catch it!

## Making time

10 mins

### Butterflies

*You will need: stiff paper, paints, paintbrushes, scissors. The children need aprons and to have their sleeves rolled up; the floor and tables should be covered. Ensure children have easy access to washing facilities and have damp cloths near the craft area to wipe off the worst.*

Here are two ways of painting butterflies.

1 Fold a piece of stiff paper in half. Draw one side of a butterfly, using the fold as the line of the body. Cut round the wings and open out so you have a butterfly shape. Show the children some photos of butterflies and point out how one side of

the wings is similar to the other. Set out a range of bright paints and let the children paint their own butterflies.

2 Give each child a piece of paper which has been folded in half and opened out again. Show them how to blob colours on one half of the paper only. Fold the paper over and press down. When opened out again, there will be a mirror pattern. Leave these to dry and then cut into a butterfly shape.

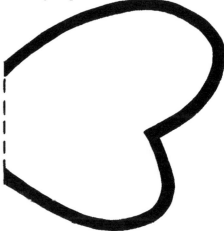

## Story time

10 mins

### God makes small animals

*You will need: any animal toys or pictures that you have used (or intend to use) during your session. Share these round so everyone has some sort of small creature to hold while you tell the story.*

In the beginning of the world – before anybody knew anything about the world – God was very busy. God was very pleased with everything he had made. God's world made him very happy. God looked at everything he had made so far and said, 'I think my light looks marvellous. My land looks just right. My sun is brilliant, just brilliant. My moon is fantastic. My stars are incredible. My plants are amazing. My big animals have turned out to be wonderful. I am so happy.'

He stroked some of the big animals and watched them move happily around his world.

'They are very big,' he said. 'Yes, they are very big. I wonder ... I just wonder...'

And then God had a 'little' idea. 'Small animals! I need small animals. They would look wonderful in my world. I need to make small animals.'

God was so pleased with his new idea. He smiled as he thought about his plans. 'I will make small animals with long fur and short fur. I will have ones that look nervous and shy. I will even have some that look gentle and kind. Oh... and I could have some animals that look so amazing, strange yet wonderful! Some will fly, some will crawl, some will scuttle on the ground, some will climb in the trees. Some of my small animals will move fast, like the wind. And some will move slowly and silently. Lots and lots of small animals! The more the better! It really will be so good.'

Straight away, God set about making small animals. He made so many because he had so many ideas for how small animals could look and live in his world. Here are the names of a few he made: squirrels, rabbits, cats, mice, gerbils and guinea pigs – beetles, caterpillars, spiders, ants, frogs, stick insects, snails. Which small animals have you got? *(Invite the children one at a time to show the animal they are holding: what sort is it?)*

'They look grand!' God whispered, in a little small voice. 'The small animals are just what I needed.' And God was so pleased with them all!

## Rhyme time

**Once I saw...**
*This rhyme can go on for as long as you can bear it! After the first couple of verses, invite the children to suggest other animals that they have seen which can be added into the rhyme.*

One, two, three, four, five,
Once I saw a bee with my eyes,
Six, seven, eight, nine, ten,
Then I saw it go again.

One, two, three, four, five,
Once I saw a dog with my eyes,
Six, seven, eight, nine, ten,
Then I saw it go again.

## Song time

**How many animals can you see?**
*You will need: an example of each animal mentioned in the song. You can always change the song to match your animals!*

*Sing (roughly!) to the tune of 'The animals went in two by two'. Help the children to count along with you.*

How many animals can you see?
    One – two – three.
Can you count them along with me?
    One – two – three.
How many animals can you see?
*The cat, the mouse and the bat –*
I can count them – one, two, three.

How many animals can you see?
    One – two. Three – four.
Can you count them along with me?
    One – two. Three – four.
How many animals can you see?
*Rabbit, worm, duck and butterfly –*
I can count them – one, two, three, four.

How many animals can you see?
    One – two. Three, four, five.
Can you count them along with me?
    One – two. Three, four, five.
How many animals can you see?
*Spider, rat, guinea pig, fox and beetle.*
I can count them – one, two, three, four, five.

## Pray time

**Pray and sing**
*You will need: an animal 'feature' for each child to wear: headband with ears or antennae attached, clip-on tail, flappy wings with loops to hold on the arms, face masks, etc.*

Invite the children to stand up one at a time: when they do so everyone says, 'Thank you God for small animals.' This prayer could be extended by asking children to say what is so special about each of the small animals and adding that to the general prayer.

Sing 'The butterfly song' together (*KS,*128, and other collections).

*Pray:*

Dear Father God

Thank you for making small animals. We really like them. Please help us to look after them as you would like us to. Amen.

## Extra time

•Arrange a well-supervised expedition to do some pond-dipping or collect and view mini-beasts. Always treat all creatures with care and return them to their original surroundings after you have observed them.

•Enjoy *The Very Hungry Caterpillar, The Bad-tempered Ladybird, The Mixed-up Chameleon* or *The Very Busy Spider,* all by Eric Carle, Puffin books.

## Adults too

Continue discussions concerning conservation and the pros and cons of zoos. (See preparations for discussing conservation issues from outline 8.) Try to encourage discussions about why some animals have become extinct. How did God manage to arrange for all the animals to have sufficient food on the earth? People might remember seeing Jurassic Park or one of the sequels: what were the issues raised there? Open discussion really helps everyone feel a part of the group, so ensure that everyone has an opportunity to contribute to discussion. Adults may well wish to talk about their experiences of small animals – particularly wild ones. Perhaps they have looked after a baby bird – or had their kitchen invaded by ants! This can generate genuine conversation.

## Top tip

Involving children in Story time, Song or Rhyme time is useful for holding their attention and for reinforcing a learning point. Children often enjoy hearing a short story more than once, especially if they are involved in some way. Read or tell the story twice if you think it is appropriate – or vary their involvement: perhaps the children can tell you part of the story. It is amazing how much they can remember!

**ACTIVITY PAGE:**
The photocopiable activity page for this outline is on page 42

## 10 God's wonderful world

# God made people

Genesis 1:27–31; Psalms 104; 148

## Play time

### Role play
*You will need: dolls, teddies and cuddly toys; a range of dressing-up clothes (saris, tabards, hats, gloves, dresses – not too long, aprons, bags); toy buggies and prams, cots and blankets. Create a home area using large boxes made into washing machine, cooker, etc. Children are very good at imagining and do not need the items to be identical to the real thing: it's the impression that counts. Add bean-bag seating or small chairs.*

Create an area where children can have access to a range of simple dressing-up clothes. Hang the clothes up or display them as well as possible to make them appealing.

Create a home area where children can play freely with all the 'home' toys. Be sure that the home area looks attractive and welcoming: this doesn't mean that lots of money needs to be spent, just lots of imagination and creativity! Allow children to play freely but intervene if there are squabbles concerning the sharing of toys. Encourage the children to rotate and share equipment. Take part in the play yourself and enter into their dialogue – children will enjoy it if you take part in the pretending.

*Be safe!* Be sure that clothes are not so long as to trip children up. Avoid high-heeled shoes as these can be very dangerous. Always be concerned for the children's safety and that means constant vigilance and supervision. Try to cultivate a practice of constantly looking around the room even whilst you interact with the children.

## Game time

### God made me
*You will need: six large cards showing different parts of the body. (Photographs if possible.) This game can be played to help children identify parts of their body as well as being great fun!*

Tell the children that one by one you are going to show them different cards. As soon as they see the card they must touch the correct part of their body and shout 'God made me!'

Children might like to take it in turns to be the one deciding which card to show.

### Pass the parcel
Prepare the parcel with a little picture and a note saying, 'Jesus loves you' within each layer of wrapping. Take time to explain at the start that the parcel contains something for everyone, not just for the child who unwraps it. (For example, a packet of biscuits. Check for allergies first before offering children anything to eat.)

## Making time

### Painted stones
*You will need: some large rounded pebbles; thick poster paint in several colours; paint brushes.*

*Before you start, cover tables, roll up sleeves and put on aprons. Children will need to be able to wash and dry their hands after this activity.*

Set out stones and palettes of thick paint on the table. Encourage the children to paint their own designs on the stones. Place a piece of paper with the name of each child next to each finished stone, while it dries.

### People faces
*You will need: paper plates or card circles, crayons, knitting wool, buttons, PVA glue, sticky tape, safety mirror.*

Talk to the children about how special God has made each one of them. They can draw their face on the plate using crayons, buttons and wool for hair.

Encourage children to look in the mirror and name their features.

## Story time

### God makes people
*You will need: the visual aids used for the previous sessions or collect pictures and items to demonstrate things God made. Put these in a shiny box and get them out as the story dictates. Involve the children in holding each item.*

'It's all so exciting!' said God. 'My world is looking wonderful! So full of colour and life!'

God went to watch the moon and was pleased with the way it shone at night. He spent time counting the stars, just to make sure they were all there. And they were. Then, he checked on the sun to make sure it was bright enough and giving out all the light needed. And it was. He walked through the forests and the gardens. All the plants were growing well. God watched the birds flying. He made sure the water was just right for all the fish. And it was. Next, God went to see the big animals to make sure they had enough to eat and were playing happily. They were. God searched around for all the small animals he had made to check if they were happy. And they were.

'What a world!' said God with great excitement. 'It is exactly as I wanted it. No mistakes – nothing wrong – all working well. Of course, it will need looking after day by day.'

And, that is when God had his gigantic thought. His best thought. His biggest thought.

'I need people,' he said very loudly. 'People will be able to look after my world. Yes, day by day, they will need to make sure everything is exactly as it should be.' So, God set about making people, the first people on the earth. He took great care in making people because they are so special. He wanted people to be just like himself.

And very soon… 'Finished!' said God. 'Here are the first people on my earth: a man and a woman.' God made sure that the people knew how to look after his world.

'Please care for my land, my plants and all my fish and birds and animals,' God asked them.

'We will,' said the man and the woman.

God was so happy that he danced around his world with a big smile on his face. 'Marvellous,' said God. 'Just right. I am very pleased. Look at my people! They are just like me! They are wonderful! It's all wonderful!' God had worked so hard. But everything was just as he wanted it to be. Then God went for a really good rest.

And that was the beginning of the world.

## Rhyme time

   10 mins

### Everyone's different
*How many sorts of people can you count in this rhyme?*

Whether I'm big
Or whether I'm small,
Whether I'm short,
Or whether I'm tall,
I am precious to Jesus.

Whether I'm thin,
Or whether I'm fat,
Whether I'm quiet,
Or whether I chat,
I am precious to Jesus.

Whether I'm young,
Or whether I'm old,
Whether I'm scared,
Or whether I'm bold,
I am precious to Jesus.

Whether I'm slow,
Or whether I'm fast,

Whether I'm first,
Or whether I'm last,
I am precious to Jesus.

Everyone's different,
No one's the same,
A different shape,
A different name,
But everyone's precious to Jesus.

## Song time

    5–10 mins

### God made you
*This song invites action and involvement: enjoy singing and moving to the tune of 'If you're happy and you know it'.*

If God made you and you know it,
    nod your head, *etc.*

If God made you and you know it,
    clap your hands…

If God made you and you know it,
    jump and hop…

If God made you and you know it,
    blink your eyes…

If God made you and you know it,
    shout, 'Praise God!'…

If God made you and you know it,
    do all five…

## Pray time

    10 mins

### I am special
*You will need: a safe play mirror.*

*Help the children to take it in turns to look in the mirror and say 'I am special to God.' (It is best if an adult starts off first.) Tell them how precious they are and that God thinks they are wonderful! Encourage children to join in singing 'Two little eyes to look to God' (quiet) or 'Everyone matters to Jesus' (active). Both songs are in JU. Tell the children you are going to say a short prayer and they can say 'Amen' at the end:*

Dear Father God,
Thank you that you made us so special and that you love us. Thank you for our eyes, ears, mouth and feet. Help us to love you too.                    Amen.

## Extra time

•Read *Adam and Eve,* Collect-a-Bible Story series, SU.

•Small world play.

•Allow children to play freely using a home-made puppet theatre and hand or stick puppets.

•See some of the children God made in *Children Just Like Me,* Dorling Kindersley.

•God made you: enjoy being you as you sing 'Playing, running, skipping, jumping' *JU,* p32.

•Let children practise writing their names.

## Adults too

Discuss with the adults some interesting facts you have found out about the human body. A trip to the library to research these facts will be worthwhile. You can present the information as you wish, perhaps by providing hand-outs or through a video. It is fascinating to think that the very hairs on our head are numbered by God and that God says he will look after us (Matthew 10:29–31).

Discuss and share times when you have felt God care for you personally. You could talk about how God has looked after you, or maybe a friend or relative. Sharing your faith can be natural and spontaneous, talking to people openly about how you have experienced God's care. Don't be afraid to admit when things did not work out perfectly: people are always fascinated to hear real-life stories and an honest account will always have an impact.

## Top tip

It is important to try to learn the children's names and to remember details about their pets or anything that they might have told you which is important to them. Talking to the children about their pets or favourite things, as well as remembering details about them, helps children to feel welcome and wanted.

**ACTIVITY PAGE:**
The photocopiable activity page for this outline is on page 43

# God made little animals.

Press your fingertip on an ink or paint pad. Make fingerprints all over the page. Wait for the prints to dry. Draw on some lines and dots to make little animals. There are some ideas already on the page.

Genesis 1:24–26; Psalms 104: 14

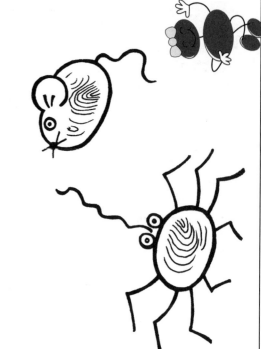

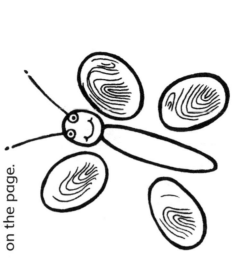

My name

Genesis 1:27
–31; Psalms
104; 148

God made people.

# Babies – John

Luke 1: 5–80

## Play time

no limit

*Include boys and girls equally in these activities. Avoid using language which indicates these are 'girls' games'.*

### Fun with babies

*You will need: dolls and baby equipment.*

Prepare a play-nursery using baby dolls and relevant dolls' equipment: prams, cots, feeding chairs, bottles, blankets and clothes. If these items are not available, provide shoe boxes for cots; and towels and strips of material as blankets. Real baby items could be used as well: baby bottles, toys, empty cereal boxes, baths, rattles. Invite the children to come into the nursery and pretend to be looking after their babies.

### Dough babies

*You will need: play dough, rolling pins, cutters (optional).*

Show the children how to make balls of dough and then shape them into babies. Encourage children to keep their work on a plastic mat. Rolling pins and gingerbread people cookie cutters may also be used to shape babies.

Dough play is a very useful activity for insecure children as it provides a wonderful outlet to release emotions and express creativity.

### Picture babies

*You will need: suitable magazine pictures of babies pasted onto thin cardboard and cut out.*

Let the children play with the 'babies' on a blanket or table. Use flannel graph boards and baby shapes if available.

### Puzzle babies

Set out simple jigsaw puzzles of families and babies (humans and other animals). Draw or paste suitable pictures on to card, cut into 2, 4 or 6 pieces and let the children assemble them. Play a matching game with toy farm or zoo animals where the child pairs up an adult and young animal.

## Game time

up to 20 mins

### Roll and crawl

*You will need: clean splinter-free floor, obstacles, jelly baby sweets (check these are suitable for vegetarians. You could make gingerbread babies instead, but check for allergies), background music.*

Tell the children they are going to pretend to be babies. Ask them to lie down. They cannot sit, crawl or walk. Ask them to roll over and over to cross the room. This game is fun to play outside on grass, especially if there's a gentle slope to roll down.

Next, tell the children that they have grown older. Ask them to show you how they can crawl. Set up an obstacle course with tunnels to crawl through, sturdy low tables to crawl over, blankets to crawl under and hoops to crawl around.

Call the children together, still crawling, and share round baby-shaped sweets or biscuits. Play soothing music while the children sit and eat, to calm them.

## Making time

20-30 mins

### Sock babies

*You will need: old socks (one per child), newspaper or packaging material, strong elastic bands, fabric pieces, baby 'faces'*

Give each child an old sock and several squares of newspaper. Show them how to crumple the newspaper into small balls. Stuff the toe section of the sock with the newspaper or safe alternative. Create a head by wrapping a band round the sock two or three times. Stuff the rest of the sock to make a firm body. Tie a knot in the end to keep it all together. Give the children pre-cut fabric remnants to make 'blankets'. Help them wrap the babies in their blankets and to tuck in the ends

securely. Show the children how to make faces by pasting on cut-out baby faces from magazines or felt features. Paste on wool or shredded paper or sections of gentle plastic pot scourers as hair.

## Story time

10 mins

### Baby John

*You will need: three helpers dressed up as Zechariah, Elizabeth and Gabriel, using simple costumes.*

*Practise the story together beforehand so that it flows smoothly. Seat the children comfortably in front of you and talk about baby brothers and sisters. Encourage the children to tell you about babies they know. Then say you are going to tell them about a baby in the Bible called John.*

Today I'm going to tell you about two old people who wanted a baby of their own. Their names were Elizabeth and Zechariah. *(Point to Elizabeth and Zechariah as they move slowly across the room. They have very sad faces.)*

Do you think they were happy or sad? *(Children respond.)*

Yes, they were very sad. You see, they had prayed and prayed, and asked God for a baby. But they still didn't have one.

Zechariah was a priest. One day he was alone in the temple. The temple was God's special house. Zechariah was doing his work for God. He was burning incense, which has a lovely smell. *(Zechariah potters around in front of the children. He gets a fright and jumps as Gabriel appears next to him.)* The angel Gabriel came and spoke to Zechariah.

Gabriel said, 'Don't be frightened,

Zechariah. God sent me to tell you that he has heard your prayers. You and Elizabeth are going to have a baby boy. Call him John. God has an important job for him. He'll tell the people to get ready for Jesus.' But Zechariah did not believe Gabriel because he thought that he and Elizabeth] were too old to have a baby.

Gabriel said, 'You don't believe me, so you will not speak again until your baby has been born.' Zechariah left the temple and went home to Elizabeth. He could not speak. *(Elizabeth speaks to Zechariah and he replies with gestures.)*

The angel's words came true. Elizabeth had a baby boy. *(Elizabeth rocks a baby doll.)*

She told everyone, 'His name is John.'

'John?' asked the people. 'Are you sure?'

Zechariah couldn't speak but he could write the answer down. He wrote 'His name is John.'*(Zechariah writes on a small board.)*

Then Zechariah was able to speak again. He was very happy. Elizabeth was very happy. They thanked God for their baby boy. God had done what he said he would do. God had kept his promise. God always keeps his promises.

## Rhyme time

### Rock your babe
*Pretend to rock a baby to this rhyme.*

Elizabeth, rock your babe,
　　rock your babe,
He is in your care.
We're praising, praising, praising God,
For he has answered prayer.

Elizabeth, rock your babe,
　　rock your babe,
Call your sweet son 'John'.
We're praising, praising, praising God,
He'll make John big and strong.

Elizabeth, rock your babe,
　　rock your babe,
Gabriel was right.
We're praising, praising, praising God,
For John is your delight.

Elizabeth, rock your babe,
　　rock your babe,
Now Zechariah sing.
We're praising, praising, praising God,
For Jesus will be king.

## Song time

### A baby for Elizabeth
*This song may be sung (loosely) to the tune of 'Mary had a little lamb'.*

Elizabeth was very sad,
　　very sad, very sad.
Elizabeth was very sad,
　　she longed for a baby.

Zechariah prayed to God, ...
　　he longed for a baby.

The angel came with special news, ...
　　they would have a baby.

Zechariah couldn't speak, ...
　　until they'd had their baby.

Baby John was born to them, ...
　　God's special messenger.

Everyone was happy then, ...
　　thank you God.

## Pray time

### Babies
*Ask the adults to sit in a circle with the children and any babies in the group. Look sad and ask the children to make sad faces too. Say, 'Elizabeth's face was sad like this because she didn't have a baby.' Repeat for Zechariah. Make happy faces and say, 'Elizabeth's face was happy like this when God sent baby John.' Repeat for Zechariah. Suggest, 'Zechariah and Elizabeth thanked God for their baby. We can thank God for our babies.' If you have babies present, ask their carers to show them to the group. Explain who the baby is, eg 'This is Kayleigh, she's Emily's baby sister.' Say together: 'Thank you God for baby Kayleigh.' Repeat for all the babies. If there aren't any baby brothers and sisters at the group, show some photos and chat a little about babies known to the children. You can either say a general prayer of thanks for all babies or mention each child's siblings by name.*

## Extra time

•Read *Welcome the baby Jesus* by Maggie Barfield, SU.

•Lie on the carpet and listen to lullabies or soothing music.

## Adults too

### Who's the baby?
Plan ahead and ask the adults to bring pictures of themselves as babies. Display these on a table or notice board, with a code number. (Take care not to damage the photos.)

Give the adults paper and pencil and encourage them to identify the babies and write down the names. Make this enjoyable: they can work together and even ask each other for clues. Have some fun prizes too. The game will also work with pictures of the children currently in the group, comparing them with pictures of them as newly born babies: they may have changed a lot in a few years.

Make this a starting point for discussing how your church marks the birth of a child. Arrange for a minister or children's group leader to come along who can explain what goes on in the church for under-fives, their families and friends.

Be aware! You may find that everyone knows each other as someone else's grandma or childminder, rather than as themselves. How can you shift this perception so you meet as people?

## Top tip

Ruth says, 'God created children with wonderful imaginations. I teach in a nursery school and often see the children folding up their sweaters to resemble a baby wrapped in a blanket. They play happily with them and show them off with pride. These "babies" give their little makers much more pleasure than expensive baby dolls. Pack away all the toys sometimes and encourage the children to have fun using their imaginations.'

**ACTIVITY PAGE:**
The photocopiable activity page for this outline is on page 48

# 12 God gives us people

# Children – Joash

2 Kings 11

no limit

### Find them!
*You will need: large containers (sand or water trays, large buckets or bins); 'filling' such as fir cones, shredded paper, dry fallen leaves, wood shavings, cardboard rolls, polystyrene packaging shapes (not the very small type which tend to cling to everything with static electricity); items to hide such as plastic figures or play people, plastic farm or zoo animals (count them so that you can check that you have them all at the end of the session).*

Fill your containers to one-third with any of the suggested fillings. Encourage the children to plunge their hands into the containers and just enjoy the feel and texture of the play medium.

Hide the plastic figures in the containers and encourage the children to find them and then hide them again. Allow the children to build, tunnel and manipulate the play medium as they wish, the only rule being to keep it in the container!

### Hiding in the leaves
If it is autumn, the children can gather clean dry leaves from the ground and make a huge pile. Then they take it in turns to hide a toy in the leaves for their friends to find. The children can also hide by covering themselves with leaves. (Make sure they are wearing old clothes and that their parents and carers are aware of the activity.)

### Hiding in the boxes
Obtain cardboard packaging boxes of varying sizes. These are usually readily available from supermarkets, etc. Allow the children to play with them – they will usually know exactly what they want to do with them! They may use them to build houses or hiding places. They may sit in them and push or pull each other around the room. They may stack them into towers which they knock down and rebuild with great delight.

15-25 mins

### Where's Joash?
Tell the children that they are going to pretend to be a little boy called Joash hiding in the temple. Choose a confident child to be the finder. All the children hide, while the finder sits on a blanket and closes his or her eyes. An adult helper can tell the finder when they can open their eyes. The finder calls 'I'm coming, Joash' and tries to find the children, while they try to run to the finder's blanket and sit down without being seen.

### Where's your crown?
*You will need: a crown from the dressing-up box.*

Ask a child to be Joash and leave the room (with an adult helper) while his crown is hidden. Call Joash to come and look for his crown. The children must not speak, but they can help Joash by clapping loudly when he is close to the hiding place and softly if he looks in the wrong place.

20-30 mins

### Happy children

*You will need: a paper plate for each child and the collage or craft items listed below.* Give each child a paper plate and then help them to make a happy face. Use one of the following methods:

• Paint the features using pre-mixed paints.
• Use a glue stick to paste on pre-cut paper shapes as eyes, ears, lips, etc.
• Provide an assortment of collage items, eg buttons, bottle tops in different sizes and colours, different pasta shapes, short lengths of wool or braid.

### Eat your face!
*You will need: plain biscuits with icing and sweets suitable for making facial features.*

Let the children assemble and then eat their faces! (Be careful to check for food allergies and be aware of health and hygiene rules.)

15 mins

### God keeps Joash safe
*You will need: flannel graph board (see Top tip) and pictures of Joash. Make eight pictures showing Joash as a baby, and then growing bigger from one to seven years old. (Or make card pictures and display them using sticky tack to hold them to a board.) Make a sparkling crown for the seven-year old Joash.*

*Chat with the children about how old they are. Explain that this Bible story is about a boy who was a little bit older than them!*

God loves children. You are all special and he loves you all. He loves all the babies, all the one year olds… *(include the age of all the children present).*

God made a baby prince. His name was Joash. *(Show baby Joash picture.)* His daddy was a king, so Joash was a prince. One day his daddy died. Joash had a wicked grandmother. She wanted to be the queen. Joash was not safe. If his nasty grandmother found him, she would hurt him.

God made sure Joash was safe. Joash's auntie took Joash to God's special house, the temple. Joash's uncle was in the temple. He would look after Joash and hide him from the unkind queen. *(Put baby Joash at the left of the board.)*

Joash's auntie and uncle hid him in the

temple for six years. They taught him all about God. God kept Joash safe. *(As you continue, add the 'growing' Joash figures from left to right so that the children can see him growing bigger. Encourage everyone to say the refrain with you.)*

When Joash was a baby, his auntie took him to the temple. *God kept him safe.*

When Joash was one, he hid in the temple. *God kept him safe.*

When Joash was two, he slept in the temple. *God kept him safe.*

When Joash was three, he ate in the temple. *God kept him safe.*

When Joash was four, he played in the temple. *God kept him safe.*

When Joash was five, he learnt about God in the temple. *God kept him safe.*

When Joash was six, he still hid in the temple. *God kept him safe.*

But when Joash was seven, Joash left the temple. *God kept him safe.*

Joash's uncle put a crown on Joash's head. *(Add crown.)* He said to the people watching, 'Joash is your king.' Everyone was very happy. They clapped their hands and shouted. 'Long live the king!'

## Rhyme time

### Joash

Joash has to stay
In the temple today.
Joash has to stay
In God's own house each day.

Joash has to play
In the temple today.
Joash has to play
In God's own house each day.

Joash has to pray
In the temple today.
Joash has to pray
In God's own house each day.

He's the king, hooray,
Joash is king today.
People clap and say,
'Joash is king, hooray.'
Three cheers for Joash!
Hip, hip, hooray!
Hip, hip, hooray!
Hip, hip, hooray!

## Song time

### God helps us

*Sing to the tune of 'If you're happy and you know it'. Use actions where appropriate, eg clap hands in the second verse.*

God is with us when we're frightened,
Yes he is!
God is with when we're frightened,
Yes he is!
God is with us when we're frightened,
God is with us when we're frightened,
God is with us when we're frightened,
Yes he is!

So we clap our hands and praise him,
Yes we do…

God will help us when we need him,
Yes he will…

So we stamp our feet and praise him,
Yes we do…

God protects us when we ask him,
Yes he does…

## Pray time

### Keep us safe

*You will need: bean bag (or soft ball).*

*Sit in a circle with the children. Talk briefly about how God kept Joash safe. Explain that we're going to pray together and ask God to keep us safe. Then we're going to say thank you because God hears our prayers.*

*Throw a bean bag to a child and when the child has caught it, pray together with the children, 'Please keep (name) safe. Thank you.' Demonstrate this with a helper first. Make sure that every child has a turn. Throw the bean bag into the smaller children's laps so that they do not miss it.*

*In closing pray,*

Our Father God,
Thank you for looking after us all and keeping us safe.          Amen.

## Extra time

•Make and/or decorate gingerbread people with icing and cake decorations.

•Paint the 'temple' walls by painting the outside walls with very large paintbrushes and buckets of water.

## Adults too

What can you do to help children in need? There may be natural links from the group, eg respite care for children with disabilities, refuges, local charities and campaigns. Or there are many charities which work internationally to help children in deprived and dangerous situations. Find out about some of these or invite someone to a social evening to tell you more about the work. Organise a fund raising event or do something practical to help.

Parents and carers are often naturally interested in children's issues. Find out about the United Nations Convention on the Rights of the Child. This incorporates the full range of human rights – civil, political, economic, social and cultural rights – of all children under the age of 18 years. The Convention's four guiding principles are:

•Non-discrimination (article 2)
•Best interests of the child (article 3)
•Survival and development (article 6)
•Participation (article 12)
For full details check your local library or log on to www.unicef.org.crc

## Top tip

Make a 'flannel graph' by covering one side of a thick piece of cardboard with felt. Make pictures by drawing (or tracing) and colouring figures using fibre tip or ballpoint pens on Vilene interfacing material (make sure you use the sort without the iron-on backing). Cut these out, press them onto the flannel graph and they will cling to it. Arrange your pictures in order and then stick them on the flannel graph as appropriate during your story. You can find many biblical pictures in *How to Cheat at Visual Aids*, SU which can be used in this way.

**ACTIVITY PAGE:**
The photocopiable activity page for this outline is on page 49

The baby's name was 'John'.

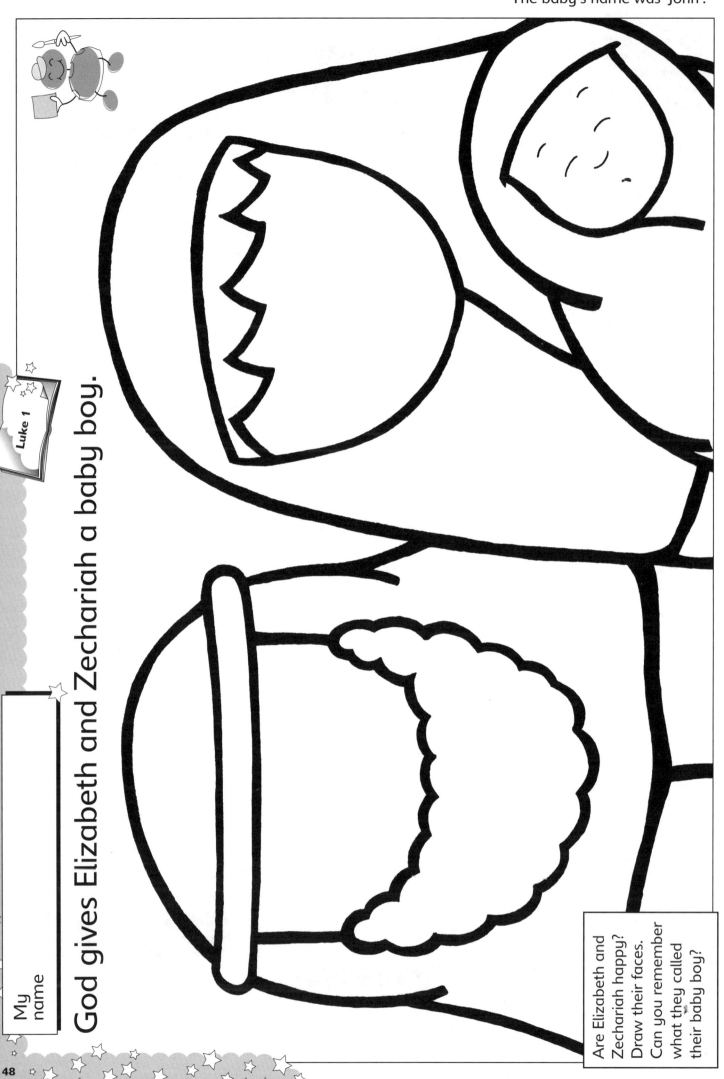

Luke 1

My name

God gives Elizabeth and Zechariah a baby boy.

Are Elizabeth and
Zechariah happy?
Draw their faces.
Can you remember
what they called
their baby boy?

# God cares for children.

2 Kings 11

God loves all these children. And God loves you! Draw yourself in the space.

My name

God loves

# Friends – Jonathan

1 Samuel 18–20

### Play time

### Friends in the quiet corner

*Set up a quiet corner for free play using some of these options:*

• Simple puzzles with pictures of children playing or working together,
• Floor puzzle that two children can make,
• Board books and picture books with friendship themes,
• Doll's house with small dolls (friends),
• Puppets of boys and girls. Also animal puppets such as dogs and cats, as children often regard their pets as friends,
• Felt boards with felt children, toys, etc, or pre-cut shapes that can be used to make pictures of friends,
• Cardboard dressing dolls with outfits.

### Come to my house

*You will need: equipment for making dens – blankets, towels, pegs, rope.*

Give the children an assortment of equipment to construct dens. They will need lengths of rope strung across the room at child height, or pieces of furniture (chairs, tables, screens) to put the pegs on.

Tell them that their friends are coming to visit and that they have to make a house or tent so that they have somewhere to sleep. They do this by pegging up the fabric to make walls, learning to work together: one child may hold one part of the house while the other pegs.

### Time for tea

*You will need: dressing-up clothes.*

Supply a variety of shoes (but avoid high heels), handbags, jewellery and dressing-up clothes for the children to dress up ready for a tea. You will also need child-sized tables and chairs and dolls' tea sets. If the weather is good or chairs and tables are not available, provide baskets and blankets so that the children can have a pretend picnic outside. Allow older children to have a small amount of water to pour into the cups as tea and tiny biscuits to put on the plates.

### Game time

### Pass the parcel

*You will need: one or more wrapped parcels – wrap a packet of small sweets (use stickers or toys if you'd rather avoid sweets) in gift wrap and then add several more layers of paper with an individual wrapped sweet in each layer; music.*

Seat the children in a circle. Ask them to pass the parcel around as you play music. When the music stops, the child holding the parcel removes one layer of paper and eats the sweet. (Stop the music so that each child gets a turn.) Continue with the game until a child removes the final layer. Encourage this child to share their prize with their friends.

With a large number of children, make two smaller circles, so that the game does not continue for too long. Each circle has its own parcel. Have extra sweets handy for any child who does not get one.

### Making time

### Friendship tree

*You will need: a big tree trunk and branches painted on a large sheet of paper and thick paint in several colours.*

Help the children paint a happy face on their hands with the fingers as the hair. Younger children may press their hand onto a paint-filled sponge pad. Help each child to make a handprint-face 'leaf' on the friendship tree.

### Paper people

Make paper dolls to represent the friends on the friendship tree. Concertina-fold a strip of paper and draw a person (see outline 17 for pattern). Cut out the doll and then open out the paper to reveal a line of people holding hands. Cutting will be too difficult for younger children, but take time to fold and cut their dolls for them as they will enjoy them so much. Colour the dolls with crayons.

### Story time

### Special friends

*You will need: toy sword, toy bow, belt, improvised tunic and robe, harp or classical guitar music, pictures of friends (from illustrated story books, catalogues, photos).*

*If possible, play some flowing rippling music in the background throughout the story. Show children colourful pictures of friends together, eg playing with toys, laughing, helping each other, comforting one another. Encourage them to talk about these pictures and their own friends. Weave in the concept that friends are gifts from God. Then lead into the story.*

The Bible tells us about a young man called David. He played harp music like this. (Listen.) His music was so beautiful that the king said 'David, please stay here and live in the palace with me. I want you to play for me when I don't feel well.' So, David stayed in the palace and met Jonathan, the king's son. David and Jonathan liked each other very much, right away.

'Will you be my friend?' asked David.

'Yes, of course I will,' said Jonathan. 'I promise to be your friend forever.'

'I promise to be your friend too,' said David.

'I would like to give you some presents because you're my friend,' said Jonathan. 'Here are some of my clothes for you and my belt.' (Show props.) 'And my sword and bow,' said Jonathan.

'Thank you, thank you,' said David. 'I'm so glad we're friends. We're going to have lots of fun together.' So, they became the best of friends and were very happy.

David was a good soldier but the king was annoyed about that. He didn't like David being a better soldier than he was. The king wanted to hurt David.

Jonathan helped his friend David. He warned him, 'Watch out, David! My dad, the king, wants to hurt you!'

Jonathan also spoke to his father. 'David is my special friend. Promise me that you won't hurt him.' The king promised and David played his harp for the king again. *(Listen.)* But one day the king tried to hurt David again. David met his friend Jonathan secretly in a field.

'I have to go away for ever, Jonathan. It's not safe for me to stay any more.' David and Jonathan were very sad. They cried and they cried. They hugged each other tightly and said goodbye. They only ever saw each other once again, but they kept their promise to be friends. Always.

## Rhyme time

### What can you do?
*Divide the children into two groups, one for David and one for Jonathan. The two groups take turns to ask a question and the other group answers with appropriate actions.*

God made me and you,
I can jump, how about you?

God made me and you,
I can dance, how about you?

God made me and you,
I can pray, how about you?

God made me and you,
I can sing, how about you?

God made me and you,
I can love, how about you?

## Song time

### Jonathan's friend
*Sing to the tune of 'London Bridge'. The song retells the Bible story, but you might like to choose one or two verses for a shorter version.*

Jonathan had a good friend,
A good friend, a good friend.
Jonathan had a good friend,
He was David.

All the people clapped and cheered, …
Hooray, David.

So the king tried to hurt him, …
Jump, jump, David.

Jonathan spoke to his dad, …
To save David.

All was well then, for a while, …
Play, play, David.

Then the king got cross again, …
Watch out, David.

Jonathan said, 'Go and hide,' …
Run, run David.

'We'll be friends for evermore, …
Good-bye David.'

## Pray time

### Friends!
*Recap the Bible story and spend a short time discussing the children's friends and then say that we are going to talk to God and thank him for giving us friends.*

*Play a happy praise tape and let the children dance around to the music. When it stops they run and stand next to some friends. (Be careful that no child feels excluded.) When the children are still, say this prayer together with appropriate actions:*

We turn around
And loudly say,
'Thank you, Lord Jesus,
For our friends today.'

We join our hands
And softly say,
'Thank you, Lord Jesus
For our friends today.'

*Repeat the music, dancing and prayer a few times.*

## Extra time

•Read *Thank You God for all My Friends* by Kath Mellentin and Tim Wood, SU

•Fold a piece of paper in half and paint a picture of yourself on one side, fold the paper over, open it and you'll see a matching friend.

## Adults too

David and Jonathan demonstrate the quality of friendship described in Proverbs 18:24: 'Some friends don't help, but a true friend is closer than your own family.' Their friendship showed loyalty, generosity, a deep and lasting affection, trust, the willingness to take risks for each other and a shared faith in God. It may seem an unlikely starting place, but your group is where such life-long friendships can begin, grow and flourish. As carers of young children, you already have much in common. Are there other ways in which you can encourage and stimulate friendships? For those who are beginning to enquire about the Christian faith, an 'Alpha' course may be the next step. Your church or others in the area may already be running courses. If not, find the nearest one from the Alpha website www.alphacourse.org which will link you up. Encourage several people to go along together – or, better still, go with them yourself and experience the course from the 'inside'.

**More from Scripture Union:**
*Finding a Spiritual Friend*, Timothy Jones

*Friendship Matters*, David Spriggs and Darrell Jackson.

## Top tip

Young children are self-centred and are still developing social skills such as sharing, being helpful, taking turns and being considerate of others' feelings. They tend to play on their own rather than with other children. Use positive reinforcement to encourage the growth of social skills, eg, 'Jack, that was very kind of you to give some of your blocks to Michaela.' Allow the children to form friendships at their own pace and level of development.

**ACTIVITY PAGE:**
The photocopiable activity page for this outline is on page 54

# Famous people – Esther

Book of Esther

## Play time

## Game time

crowns as they wish. Allow the crowns to dry. Fit each child's individually. Staple each crown into a head-sized circle. Make sure that the bent edges of the staples are on the outside of the crown or that you tape over them so that they do not scratch or catch the children's hair.

### Sand castles
*You will need: sand (slightly damp); objects to decorate castles – bottle tops, shells, flags, pebbles, twigs.*

Sand is an ideal medium for making castles. Encourage the children to build castles in the sand pit or in sand trays using their hands and no tools. The children can decorate their castles with the objects provided. Introduce sand toys too if you wish: buckets, spades, rakes, sieves, moulds, funnels. Or try using wooden spoons, flower pots of different colours, shapes and sizes, plastic containers such as yoghurt pots and margarine tubs, little bags made out of a very loose woven fabric (sieves), biscuit cutters, washing powder scoops, funnels cut from the tops of plastic bottles, tea strainers, plastic jugs.

### Block castles
*You will need: wooden blocks.*

Children will also enjoy making castles using wooden blocks. If you do not have any blocks, try to obtain wood off-cuts from a timber merchant, furniture factory or a school or college technology department. Blocks tend to be noisy so this activity should take place on a carpet to reduce the sound level.

### Your majesty!
*You will need: crowns, jewellery, gloves, shiny shoes (but not high heels) and cloaks made from fabric remnants.*

Give the children the opportunity to pretend to be queens and kings. Make thrones by covering chairs with table cloths, small blankets and tinsel. Decorate pedal cars, trolleys or big boxes with tinsel to make coaches for processions; empty wool cones can be used as trumpets. Some children can ride hobby-horses and pretend to pull or ride alongside the coaches.

### The queen declares…
Mark a starting line and a castle line on the ground with chalk or masking tape. The children line up on the starting line and the leader calls out instructions, using a funny pompous voice, indicating how the children should move towards the castle: 'The queen declares walk backwards'. Try: rolling over and over, hopping, skipping, galloping, jumping, crawling slowly… Children move towards the castle line and then turn around and come back again. Try this a few times. If the children are enjoying this and obeying their queen, add a further instruction which the children will need to listen for. At random intervals call out, 'The queen declares STOP!' The children must stop immediately and freeze. They can only move again when the queen permits! No one need be out in this game. It's fun to play for short times, perhaps in between other activities.

## Making time

### Crowns
*You will need: card; adhesive; spreaders; brushes; scissors; decorations – paint, glitter, wax crayons, self-adhesive shapes (stars, circles, diamonds), small scraps of fabric and gift wrap, paper doilies, shiny buttons, bottle tops, coloured cellophane, shiny or metallic sweet wrappers; stapler; sticky tape.*

Make a simple template and draw crown outlines on strips of flexible cardboard. Crowns may be ready cut for younger children, but the older children may enjoy cutting their own crowns.

Provide decorative materials with appropriate tools and adhesive. Encourage the children to decorate their

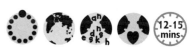
## Story time

### Queen Esther
*You will need: pictures of famous people or characters, enlarged version of the activity page.*

*Display pictures of famous characters: TV presenters, actors, singers and musicians, national leaders – anyone whom you think the children will recognise.*

*Chat together with the children about the pictures. Who is it? What do they do? Where do we see them? Show interest in the children's answers: they will give you much insight into their lives and how they understand their world. Tell Esther's story.*

Here's another famous person. Her name was Esther, which means 'star'. The Bible tells us that she was very beautiful.

Esther and her older cousin Mordecai belonged to God's special people. They were Hebrews.

The country where Esther and Mordecai lived was ruled by King Xerxes. One day King Xerxes held a party. He asked his wife Queen Vashti to go to the party. But Queen Vashti refused. So, King Xerxes told Queen Vashti to leave the palace for ever.

Now King Xerxes wanted a new queen. He called all the beautiful young girls in the country to go to the palace. He was going to choose one to be his wife. Esther was very beautiful. So Mordecai told Esther to go to the palace with all the other pretty girls. When the king saw Esther, he thought she was very beautiful. He liked her the best of all.

'Esther, you will be my new queen,' he declared. King Xerxes put a crown on her head. Now she was Queen Esther. The king didn't know Esther was a Hebrew.

There was a man in the palace called Haman. He did not like the Hebrew people. Haman wanted to get rid of them all. Esther's cousin, Mordecai, was very unhappy. He asked Queen Esther to speak to the king. He wanted the king to save all the Hebrew people.

Esther was afraid to go and speak to the king. But she wanted to help her people, so she prayed to God.

God helped her to be brave. Esther went to the king. 'I am a Hebrew,' she said, 'and Haman is trying to get rid of all the Hebrew people.'

King Xerxes listened to what Queen Esther said. Then the king made a new law. The Hebrew people were saved. They were all very happy. All because Queen Esther was brave enough to ask the king for his help.

## Rhyme time

### Curtsy and bow
*Make a line of girls and a line of boys facing each other. As they say the rhyme the girls curtsy and the boys bow at the appropriate times.*

Curtsy and bow,
All together now,
Curtsy and bow,
To Queen Esther,
Brave Queen Esther.
The prettiest queen
We've ever seen.
Curtsy and bow,
All together now,
Curtsy and bow.

*Children who wish, can take it in turns to be Esther and walk down the line between the 'subjects'!*

## Song time

### The new queen
*Sing this song to the tune of 'Frère Jacques'. Use only the last verse for the very young children.*

Old Queen Vashti, old Queen Vashti,
Would not go, would not go,
To her husband's party, to her husband's party,
Oh, no, no. Oh, no, no.

Jewish Esther, Jewish Esther,
Pretty girl, pretty girl,
Listen to your cousin, listen to your cousin,
Go to the king. Go to the king.

New Queen Esther, new Queen Esther,
Spoke to the king, spoke to the king,
She has saved her people, she has saved her people,
Thank you, God. Thank you, God.

Good Queen Esther, Good Queen Esther,
You're so brave, you're so brave,
All your people praise you, all your people praise you,
They love you. Yes they do.

## Pray time

### God our king!
*Place a crown on your head and explain that God is our heavenly father and that he is also our king! So, we are like princes and princesses. We do not need to be brave like Esther to speak to him. We can speak to him whenever we want to. We can praise him or ask for something. We can just have a chat and tell him what we've been doing. Let each child wear the crown and say a short personal prayer. If a child does not want to pray aloud, they simply pass the crown on.*

*If you have all made crowns, wear them and say this prayer together.*

Dear Father God
thank you that we can always talk to you and that you always hear us.
Amen.

## Extra time

•Play percussion instruments – improvise if you do not have instruments.

•Mix powder paints with a strong salt solution to make pictures that sparkle when dry.

•*Esther – the girl who became queen* is a 'Veggie Tales' video from Big Idea productions. (View any video before showing it to young children and check on copyright restrictions if you intend to show it to your group.)

## Adults too

We live in a culture where people crave fame – at almost any price. Fame is not dependent on great achievement or effort – you can be 'famous for being famous'. Yet many celebrities complain at the emptiness of fame, at the intrusion on their privacy and at always being a public person. Discuss what 'fame' is all about. Who do you admire in the public eye? What is it about them that attracts you? What would you like to be famous for? Pool your knowledge about famous Christians: politicians, musicians, sports people. What are the extra pressures for them? What are the pluses? And the pitfalls?

For carers of young children, this quote from the musician Sting may sound particularly poignant: 'When I was young my overwhelming ambition was to be famous. I wanted it so much so that my parents would be forced to notice me.'

## Top tip

Always treat the children as though they are royalty and make each child feel special. Greet each child by name as they arrive. Make sure that each child is affirmed with positive comments during the meeting, eg, 'That's very kind of you to help Susan.' Give your full attention to them when they talk to you and show interest in the little details of their lives that they tell you.

**ACTIVITY PAGE:**
The photocopiable activity page for this outline is on page 55

# God gives us friends.

1 Samuel 18–20

My name

Make your handprint here.

Ask your friend to make a handprint here.

My hand.

My friend's hand.

I like to share with my friend.

God helped
Queen Esther to
be brave.

Cut out the doll of Esther and
her clothes. Dress Esther to look
like a queen.

My
name

Book of
Esther

55

# People to care for us – Eli

1 Samuel 1:9–2:11 and 2:26

## Play time

no limit

### Let's be grown ups
*You will need: equipment and clothes to role play people that help us.*

**Doctors and nurses** – make a hospital corner with a child-sized bed or dolls' beds with sheets, pillows and blankets. Put out nurses' uniforms, doctors' coats, etc, for the children to wear. Provide a toy doctor's kit. The children will have fun taking care of each other or the dolls in hospital. Short lengths of real bandages will add to the fun.

**Dentists** – make a dental surgery with a folding bed or sturdy garden chair serving as the dentist's chair.

**Shop assistants** – collect empty bottles and cartons, or magazines and newspapers, or stationery items to stock a shop or post office. Let the children set up a shop on the tables or shelves that are available, or give them big boxes to make a counter and shelves. Add a toy till (or a small box to use as a till). Provide money-sized rectangles of paper and crayons for the children to make their own notes. Bottle tops or real coins of low denomination can also be used for the game. Children will also need handbags, purses, wallets and baskets to go shopping.

**Librarians** – arrange your book collection as a library. Use a table or box to make a counter for issuing books. Make some pretend books out of folded scrap paper so that the librarian can date stamp them inside – children love doing this, but make sure they only stamp the play books.

### Puppets
Put out puppets for free play. Encourage the children to play games where the puppets look after a sick, scared or lost puppet.

## Game time

10 mins

### Who cares for me?
This game will work well if you get some adults involved! They need to dress up as 'people who care for us'. Props don't need to be elaborate: a hat or an item to carry would be enough. Let them explain who they are pretending to be: 'I'm dressed up like a doctor. A doctor will care for you if you're not feeling very well.' (If real adults are not available, have large pictures of people in these roles to show.)

Gather the children in the centre of the room while the 'carers' spread out. Describe a situation, eg who cares for me when I am lost at the shops, am ill, fall over at playgroup? The children run to the right person. When they all get to the right place, they can form a ring around the carer and circle round singing to the tune of 'Here we go round the mulberry bush':

> 'Thank you now for being there,
> being there, being there,
> thank you now for being there,
> when we need some help.'

All return to the centre of the room and repeat with other carers.

## Making time

20 mins

### People who look after me

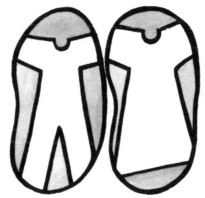

*You will need: large potatoes, knife, poster or tempera paint, shallow trays or saucers, sponge, paper. Use a sharp knife to cut several large potatoes in half. Make sure that the cut surfaces are completely flat. Cut out printing shapes (small and large) as shown.*

Take the trays and line each one with a layer of sponge or a thick wad of paper towel. Mix thick paint and pour a different colour into each tray. Show the children how to make potato prints. Ask them to make pictures of themselves and some of the people who look after them. Complete the pictures with crayons or felt tips when they are dry.

## Story time

15 mins

### People who care
*Introduce the story by discussing people who look after babies and small children. Ask questions such as, 'Who is looking after you today? Who washes your clothes? Who looks after you at home?' Keep the discussion short and lively and then let it flow into the story…*

Do you know that there was a woman in the Bible who didn't have any children of her own? Her name was Hannah. She was sad because she had asked God lots of times for a baby, but she still didn't have one. She was so sad that she cried and she cried. She didn't even want to eat.

Every year Hannah went with her husband to God's special house. This was in a place called Shiloh. They went there to tell God how much they loved him. They sang special songs for God and prayed to him.

One evening, after supper, Hannah went to God's special house in Shiloh. Once again she asked God to give her a baby boy. She promised God that if he gave her a son, she would give him back to God. A priest called Eli sat near the door and watched her pray. Afterwards he spoke to Hannah and blessed her.

This time God answered Hannah's prayer. He gave her a baby boy. She called him Samuel. She loved her baby and looked after him well. He grew big and strong. Hannah remembered her promise to God. When Samuel was old enough, she kept her promise. She took him to God's special house in Shiloh.

Samuel lived in God's special house with Eli. Eli looked after Samuel. Samuel helped Eli to do his work. Samuel grew so much that Hannah had to make him new clothes. Every year Hannah travelled to Shiloh and took a lovely new coat to Samuel.

*Ask, 'How do you think Eli took care of Samuel?' Encourage the children to make suggestions: accept their ideas and add some of your own if necessary, eg perhaps he played games with Samuel, hugged him when he hurt himself, taught him about God's love, made sure his bed was comfortable, told him stories, looked after him if he was ill, etc.*

*Finish the story with:*

Eli looked after Samuel very well. As Samuel grew up, everybody loved him very much. God was pleased with Samuel and God loved him very much, too.

## Rhyme time

    10 mins

### Looking after Samuel

*Ask one of the leaders to say Hannah's verses and let the children enjoy being Eli and answering.*

Hannah came to Eli and said,
'God answered my prayer.
He sent me a little boy.
Now I must keep my promise –
Will you keep Samuel in your care?'

(ELI) *'Yes, I'll look after your son,
We'll laugh and have lots of fun.'*

'Will you watch him at play?
Will you teach him to pray?'

*'Yes, I'll…'*

'Will you always stay near?
If he calls will you hear?'

*'Yes, I'll…'*

'Will you make sure he sleeps?
Cuddle him if he weeps?'

*'Yes, I'll…'*

'Will you sing him a song?
Make sure that he grows up strong?'

*'Yes, I'll…'*

'Thank you, Eli.'

## Song time

    10 mins

### In God's house

*Sing to the tune of 'The lion sleeps tonight'.*

In God's house,
His special house,
Sad Hannah cries tonight.
In God's house,
God's special house,
Sad Hannah cries tonight.
Oooooooooooooooooooh. Come pray to God. *(Repeat.)*
Come pray to God *(Repeat to end of tune.)*

In God's house,
His special house,
Old Eli blesses her…
Oooooooooooooooooooh…

To God's house,
His special house,
Glad Hannah brings her child…
Oooooooooooooooooooh…

In God's house,
His special house,
Old Eli cares for him…
Oooooooooooooooooooh…

In God's house,
His special house,
Young Samuel works and plays…
Oooooooooooooooooooh…

## Pray time

     10-15 mins

### God cares for me

**You will need:** *a bag of everyday items (toothbrush, spoon, pyjamas).*

*Talk about when God cares for the children. Help them to realise that God is looking after them. Take an item out of the bag (eg a spoon). Tell them that God is looking after them all the time, even when they are eating. Pass the bag around and help the children to pull items out and then use them to give instances of when God is looking after them.*

*Ask the children to repeat this prayer, phrase by phrase:*

Thank you Father God,
for looking after us
all the time.
Thank you

for giving us people
to care for us too.          Amen.

## Extra time

•Draw or paint pictures of 'someone who looks after me'.

•Make cards or paper flowers to thank the grown-ups who care for the children.

## Adults too

It's hard work taking care of young children! Parents and carers need to take time to take care of their own physical, spiritual, emotional and intellectual needs. Why not organise an interesting demonstration or informal talk to help them to do this? Make sure your speakers know the type of group and that the noise level may be quite high, even if you are in a separate area to the main play space.

Here a few suggestions:

•a talk about healthy eating – include some delicious samples to taste and hand out recipe sheets,

•an aerobics or gymnastics demonstration. (This has the potential to develop into a weekly class while the children are busy.)

•a weekly/monthly Bible study of principles relevant to the carers (relationships, bringing up children) which could develop into parenting classes,

•professional (and friendly!) advice on budgeting, adult education, health and safety, taking children on holiday, helping the environment – or any area of interest.

## Top tip

When using a circle activity such as described in this week's prayer section, expect varying responses. The confident enthusiastic children may shout out their ideas – give them their turn but do not allow them to dominate. Tell them you will listen to them afterwards – and make sure that you take the time to do so. Invite the quiet and shy children to participate, but never force them or make them feel uncomfortable or embarrassed.

**ACTIVITY PAGE:**
The photocopiable activity page for this outline is on page 60

# Jesus the teacher

John 13: 31–35

## Play time

no limit

### Book corner

Make a special book corner with cushions and rugs and lots of interesting picture books. Have an adult sitting there all the time, if possible, to look at the books and read them to children. (See Top tip.) The books could be books that focus on relationships and family love – there are many on the market, and available in libraries which feature animal families and explore the theme of giving and showing love in this context, eg, *Guess How Much I Love You* by Sam McBratney, Walker Books. Remember too that some children will have very limited experience of love, and the chance they have in this session to sit with an adult and enjoy a story or pictures together, may be a new experience for them.

### Good play

*You will need: lots of toys that encourage cooperative play. Include things that are unusual or special – painting or water play if you don't usually have them. If you can find heart-shaped beads for threading or jigsaws use these too.*

When you see children playing happily together let them know you are pleased with them. Learning to share and wait for turns is a valuable skill not just for socialising but also for showing love to others.

### The love corner

*You will need: lots of dolls and soft animal toys with clothes and beds with covers and prams, for the children to love.*

Encourage the children to dress and care for the dolls, putting them to bed and tucking them in, or taking them for a walk around the room in their prams. Talk about how parents and carers show love to their children, as the children play. You could set up a tea table for the dolls too and let the children choose what they will feed them from cut-out paper 'foods' (from magazines).

## Game time

5-10 mins

### Tangrams

*You will need: tangram puzzles cut out of stiff card in various colours*

Make very simple tangram puzzles by drawing a heart shape onto thick card and cutting it out. Cut each heart into several irregularly shaped pieces.

Do this with several cards of various colours. Muddle all the pieces up and let the children sort out their own pieces. Can they put them together to make a heart shape? You will probably have to do one first so they can see what shape it should be. Talk about how to arrange the pieces; use vocabulary such as: turn, curved edge, straight; building vocabulary as they play. Sorting, classifying and manipulating shapes are also all valuable pre-school learning objectives.

## Making time

15-25 mins

### Kind hearts

*You will need: prepared dough, baking trays or foil dishes, decorations, heart-shaped cookie cutters, rolling pins and bags to put the cookies in to take home. Be aware of health, hygiene and allergy issues.*

Make heart-shaped biscuits. Have the dough ready prepared; and use heart-shaped cutters. Do this activity near the beginning of your time if you are going to cook the biscuits, otherwise send them home to be cooked. Designate one helper as the 'cook' and make sure only that person goes near the oven.

Make a sweet dough by mixing flour with half its weight of butter or a vegetable fat. Add sugar to taste and cinnamon for flavouring. Bind the whole together with a little water to make a rolling dough. The children will enjoy rolling real dough for a change and the cookies can be decorated with sugar strands, glacé cherries, fruit pastilles or chocolate chips, or sprinkled with sugar and cinnamon.

Don't forget to take the cookies to share with the people at home that you love.

### Love bag

*You will need: pre-cut, heart-shaped felt pieces in a variety of colours and sizes; scraps of ribbon; fabric glue; sequins or similar shapes; stapler and staples; a paper napkin and cookie per child.*

Tell the children to choose two felt heart shapes the same size as each other, and a piece of ribbon. This gives valuable practice in matching and comparing skills, and also allows for vocabulary extension as you talk about colours and sizes. Dab dots of glue onto one of the shapes and let the children stick sequins on. Use a small stapler to staple the two shapes together, making a bag with the top open. Staple a ribbon handle either side of the opening. The children can then put a cookie or two into the bag, and give it to someone special.

## Story time

**Jesus the teacher**

*You will need: dolls and a toy table or box.*

*Illustrate the story by using dolls or soft toys and an upturned box for a table. Tell it like this.*

Jesus and his friends were having a special meal together. Here they are, coming to sit round the table. Here's Jesus, and Peter, and John and James. Look, this side are Philip and Matthew and Thomas, and Andrew and Bartholomew and Thaddeus and Simon. And here's Nathaniel. They enjoyed being together because they were friends. What do you think they'd like to eat? *(Have brief discussion but don't get too far off the subject.)* Maybe… But I know they had bread and some wine to drink. They talked about all sorts of things, things they'd done, places they'd been, what they were going to do. But as well as having fun together, Jesus had something very important to say to them.

'Listen,' he said. 'I'm not going to be with you much longer. I've got to go away. But remember I love you. And I want you to love each other, just like I love you. That way, everyone will know that you are my friends. So remember, I'm telling you to love one another.'

Jesus' friends thought that was very important. One of the friends, John, wrote it down, so that they'd never forget. And they promised to love each other. Jesus wants us to love each other too.

*Reinforce Jesus' message by asking, 'What did Jesus ask his friends to do?'*

## Rhyme time

**Jesus loves you!**

*Teach this simple rhyme which tells the basic concept that we are considering today.*

Jesus said, 'I love you,
Now love each other too.
Love each other, love each other,
Just like I love you.'

## Song time

**I love you and you love me**

*Teach the children this song, to the tune of 'Twinkle, twinkle little star'.*

I love you and you love me,
That's the way it's meant to be.
Jesus told us what to do,
'Love your friends like I love you.'
I love you and you love me,
That's the way it's meant to be.

*When the children know this song, stand them in a circle and sing it again adding these actions.*

Line 1: point to self and different children.
Line 2: join hands and stand still nodding head to agree.
Lines 3 and 4: hold hands and walk round slowly.
Lines 5 and 6: as lines 1 and 2.

## Pray time

**Known by name**

*You will need: a backing board with 'We are all friends' written at the top , paper slips with children's names written on them, Blu tack (or use large sticky notes).*

*Spread the names out on a low table, help children find their own and stick them on the board. Talk to each child about the shapes of the letters of their name and encourage them to recognise their name. They are very proud of being able to 'read' their own name, and it is a useful accomplishment.*

*Play a game by asking whose name you are pointing to. Then ask them to stand up when you point to their name. As each child stands, say together, 'Thank you God for… (child's name). We're glad (he or she's) our friend'.*

## Extra time

• Read *Jesus teaches*, Little Fish book, SU.

• Make heart-shaped photo frames.

• Let the children paint pictures of or for people they love.

• See *LACH*, p90, for songs and rhymes about being good friends.

## Adults too

Very often parents are confused about the relationship between love and discipline. They need reassurance that their parenting problems are not unique. Can you organise an informal evening to talk about these issues? Perhaps a discussion or Bible study on the subject? Or invite a more experienced parent to talk. This could be followed up by a parenting course, or an offer to pray regularly for family issues.

Have some of these resources available for people to borrow:

*The Sixty Minute Father; The Sixty Minute Mother* (books); *The Sixty Minute Parent* (video): Rob Parsons; *Being a Grandparent* (Jim Harding); *Sleep* (Kate Daymond); *Toddler Years* (Steve Chalke), all by Hodder and Stoughton. *All Alone? Help and Hope for Single Parents*, Paternoster Publishing.

For parenting support, events and advice groups based in the UK contact: Care for the Family, PO Box 488, Cardiff CF15 7YY. Telephone: 029 2081 0800. Website: www.careforthefamily.co.uk. The Christian Family Network www.cfnetwork.co.uk is a multimedia resource for Christian families which has a membership subscription and provides a great variety of helpful material and contacts.

## Top tip

Sometimes we want to teach Bible concepts, not only stories. Jesus' command to his followers to 'love one another' is like this. Children experience love in doing things together and having fun, in cuddles and shared times. We can't 'teach' them love but we can demonstrate loving attitudes and behaviour towards them. The children will learn what loving each other means as week by week we care for them, share special times with them and help them to enjoy each others' company too.

**ACTIVITY PAGE:**
The photocopiable activity page for this outline is on page 61

# God gives us people to care for us.

Help Samuel to put on his new coat. Stick pieces of coloured fabric or paper on to Samuel to give him a new coat to wear.

1 Samuel 1:9–2:11 and 2:26

My name

# Jesus said, "Love one another."

John 13: 31-35

Draw a circle round the children who are loving.

# 17 Let's find out about Jesus

# Jesus the healer

*Luke 17: 11–19*

## Play time

### Count, sort and match

*You will need: items to count such as large beads, buttons, blocks, cotton reels, puzzle trays, stacking toys, matching games.*

Many toys can be used to develop ideas of matching, belonging, sets and counting. It would be good if you ensure that any activities which can be used this way involve an adult to encourage the children to count how many, find the matching ones, thread ten beads and so on. Even building towers to knock down again can be counting exercises. Setting a table for a doll's tea party also gives counting and matching practice.

### Let's count

*You will need: beads or cotton reels; lengths of thread with the end tied in a large knot, rather than round a bead; thick blunt needles which will pass through the beads you have chosen, or shoelaces with plastic ends.*

Threading gives an opportunity for counting and matching. Ask the children to thread different amounts of different colours. Encourage them to count up to five only at this stage (see Top tip).

### Hospitals

*You will need: a hospital consisting of dolls in beds; a play doctor's kit including medicine, bandages, and plasters.*

Children will love to pretend to be the doctor and take temperatures and give medicine to the toys in the hospital.

## Game time

### Following on

*You will need: a clear space with defined limits.*

This is an opportunity for the children to do lots of moving about and work off some energy! All hold hands in a line sideways along one side of the space or room. Walk forward one step at a time and count how many steps it takes to get from one side to the other. Is it the same when we come back the other way?

Tell the children that in today's story some people went to find Jesus. We're going to pretend to be those people. Still holding hands, but following each other now, let one child be the leader and lead the others wherever they want. After a while let someone else be the leader. You could have several 'chains' of children weaving in and out amongst each other, particularly if you have an adult as the leader. Children find this great fun.

## Making time

### Ten men

*You will need: round sticky labels, crayons, paper strips at least ten times as long as the diameter of the labels. (Have sticky tape ready for emergency repairs.)*

The children are going to make a zigzag strip of the ten men in a similar way to the zigzag dolls you will make for Story time. Prefold the paper strip for them and then unfold it. Show them how to stick a face on each section, and give it eyes and a mouth. Now, when the paper is spread out you can see all the ten men that Jesus made better, but when you fold it up there is only the one who came back to say thank you! Sticking and folding are difficult for tiny fingers, but this is a good way of getting some practice in.

## Story time

### Jesus the healer

*You will need: a cardboard cut-out picture of Jesus; paper folded and drawn to make a string of ten paper dolls. (If you find the scissors won't go through ten layers, make shorter strings and tape them together.)*

*As you start your Story time, you should be cutting out a string of paper dolls. Show the children how your single doll unfolds to become – how many? Count to ten as you unfold. You will use the dolls to represent the men with leprosy. (Be careful how you talk about leprosy: avoid describing it as a skin disease as the story may distress children with eczema.) Now tell the story like this.*

These ten people were very ill. Nobody could make them better. The other people said to them, 'Go away, out of our town. We don't want to get ill like you. Go away and don't come near us.' So they went away, very sadly.

One day they heard that Jesus had come to town. *(Stand up your figure of Jesus.)* They went to see him, but they were still scared of the other people and so they stayed a long way away. *(Hold up your string of dolls.)* The ten men shouted as loud as they could, 'Jesus, master, have pity on us.'

Jesus looked at them. 'Go and see the priest,' he said. *(Explain that in those days, that's what you did to show that you were better.)*

The ten men turned away and went towards the priest's house. As they went, they felt better. The ten men looked at each other. They looked better too. They knew Jesus had made them well.

One of them tore himself away from the others *(Tear off one paper doll.)* and rushed back to Jesus, shouting at the top of his voice, 'I'm well. Thank God, Jesus made me well.' This one man ran right up to Jesus and knelt at his feet. 'Thank you, thank you, Jesus,' he said. Jesus looked at him. 'Weren't there ten of you?' he said. 'Where are the others?' Then Jesus smiled. 'You're healed because you trusted me,' he told the one man. 'Go and be well.'

*Note:* young children are sometimes quite indignant about this story. Be prepared for some strong reactions to the nine men who didn't come back!

## Rhyme time

(7-10 mins)

### Finger fun
*This is a finger play rhyme, which will help the children begin to understand the meaning of ten. They will have fun trying to move their fingers one at a time.*

One, two, three, four, five,
Fingers on one hand.
One, two, three, four, five
Fingers on the other.
But if I count them both at once
Well then,
I've got one, two, three, four, five, six, seven,
Eight, nine, ten.

*The Bible story is retold in 'Ten sick men', LACH, p56.*

## Song time

(10 mins)

### Ten sick people
*Hold up fingers and thumbs of both hands to represent the ten men who were healed. In each verse, fold down one finger, until only one remains. Allow enough time between verses for the children to sort their fingers out – some digits are harder than others to fold down! Sing to the tune of 'Ten green bottles'.*

Ten sick people ask for Jesus' help,
Ten sick people ask for Jesus' help,
And if one healed person
        runs away and hides,
There'll be nine sick people
        to ask for Jesus' help.

*Count down till only one man/finger remains. Sing:*

One sick person asks for Jesus' help,
One sick person asks for Jesus' help,
And if one healed person
        comes and thanks the Lord
There'll be no sick people
        to ask for Jesus' help.

### Other songs
'Jesus' hands were kind hands', *KS*, 194

'You are the best', *KS*, 391

## Pray time

(8-10 mins)

### Please Jesus
*You will need: a large-scale string of paper dolls and a broad felt pen. To make the dolls large enough, cut out individual shapes from A4 paper and tape them together at the back.*

*Ask the children and their parents and carers if they know anyone who is sick and who they would like us to pray to Jesus for. Write the names on the dolls. Fold the string of dolls up and pray for each person as you unfold it and their name appears. Stick the dolls on the wall or a notice-board with the sentence, 'Jesus, please make our friends feel better'.*

*Lead this prayer and let the children join in with the last line.*

Jesus made ten people well,
But only one said thanks.
Jesus is a special friend
Thanks, thanks Jesus.

Thanks for fun and thanks for friends
Thanks for toys and games
Thanks for stories, thanks for songs
Thanks, thanks Jesus.

## Extra time

•Read *Jesus heals*, Little Fish book, SU.

•Use face paint pencils to paint faces on each finger so the children have their own ten sick people. Show them how to curl all their fingers away and just leave one thumb sticking up.

•The 'Topsy and Tim' books (Ladybird) have stories about life experiences, eg, being ill.

•Find pictures of 'people who help us when we are ill' to make a collage.

•Mime feeling ill and feeling better.

## Adults too

Could you tell the adults who stay or visit that as Christians you believe that God heals people in answer to prayer, and offer prayer, not just today, but on an ongoing basis for themselves, their children and relatives who are sick? Today's story shows the power of Jesus and also his generosity: all the men are healed, whether they remember to thank him or not. Include an offer to pray on your publicity materials and notice-board as well as verbally.

Do you know a contemporary story about God's healing? Bring in a Christian video, book or magazine that has a 'testimony' of someone who has experienced healing and use that as a conversation starter. It could be about someone well known, but it's often even more effective to share from personal or close experience. Your 'ordinary' story will have impact because it is authentic and truthful.

## Top tip

The concept of number constancy (that five is always five no matter how it's arranged) is one that small children do not have. If you have a pile of six toys spread out, they will say there are more than if they are squashed together. While some may be able to 'count' they often miss an object, or just parrot the words. So, today we are asking the impossible in considering 'ten'! However, as we have ten fingers, and most children will understand 'one', you should be able to manage. A lot of the activity today will be working towards a concept of number. Matching and making sets is a vital pre-number skill. Recognising the number names is another.

**ACTIVITY PAGE:**
**The photocopiable activity page for this outline is on page 66**

# Jesus talks to God

Matthew 6:5–14

## Play time

no limit

### Home corner
*You will need: 'home' role-play equipment – baby dolls, cooking equipment, toy tools, etc.*

Let the children play at family life. Be aware that family life is not stereotypical – children in your group will have experienced many and varied family structures and each, to them, is what is 'normal'!

### Book corner
Stories about family relationships include:

*Peace at Last* by Jill Murphy, Walker Books
*Can't you Sleep, Little Bear?* by Martin Waddell, Walker Books
*Not Like That, Like This* by Tony Bradman and Joanna Burroughes, Picture Mammoth

### Talking and listening
*You will need: toy telephones, mobile phones, radio, cassette recorder, personal CD players.*

Encourage free play with the toys. Develop this into a structured activity: encourage both children and adults to talk, sing, play instruments and record their efforts. Play the tape back so that they can enjoy listening to themselves.

### Sandwiches
*You will need: a selection of toppings, butter or margarine and bread of your choice. This could be white or brown, rolls or sliced bread. Alternatively, use pitta bread, ciabatta, baguettes or croissants and explain that these are all varieties of bread from different countries. Be aware of allergy, hygiene and safety issues.*

Ask the children to choose some bread and toppings which they would like to sample. Supervise them discreetly, as they make their own sandwiches.

## Game time

5-15 mins

### Nursery favourites
For groups with lots of space to move around, play traditional games that need the children to be very quiet: 'What's the time Mr Wolf?', 'Grandmother's footsteps', or 'Bear and the honey pot' which is played sitting in a circle. ('Bear' is blindfolded and has a pot in front of him which contains treats. A leader chooses a child to quietly creep up and take one of the treats without Bear hearing them. If Bear hears a noise, he has to point in that direction, and if he successfully points at the child, the child has to go back to their seat and someone else has a try.)

### What's that?
*You will need: a cassette recorder and recordings of familiar sounds. These could be ones often heard in the house (tap, bath water emptying, kettle boiling, toaster popping up) or ones heard outside (traffic, Pelican crossing bleeps, police car siren).*

Play the sounds back for the group to guess. This game could gently introduce the idea that prayer involves listening as well as talking.

## Making time

10-20 mins

### Prayer kites

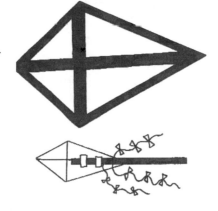

Provide coloured paper kite shapes for individual children to decorate with pictures or drawings of things for which they would like to say 'Thank you', eg, families, friends, clothes, food. Add a tail made of florists' or gift-wrapping ribbon, then tape the main part of the kite to a small stick (the kind used to support houseplants). Take the kites outside to watch the tails blow in the breeze.

Explain that we cannot see the wind but know it is there because of the effect it has on things. We can know God is there because he listens when we talk to him.

Alternatively, work as a group to make a large kite and add paper bows with prayers written on them to the tail. Display it as a wall decoration.

### Paper plate meals
Paste cut-out pictures of food onto paper plates. Write on the back of each plate 'Give us our food for today'.

## Story time

5 mins

### Jesus talks to God
*This outline is about talking to God and gives a basic introduction to prayer. Children will hear about how Jesus talked to God and how he showed others to do the same.*

Jesus was a very busy person. He liked helping people. If they were ill, Jesus could make them well again. If they were sad, Jesus would listen to them. If they wanted to ask questions, Jesus would answer them. Jesus also told lots of interesting stories so that people would understand about God, his father. Everywhere he went, crowds of people followed him. Everybody wanted to see Jesus.

But sometimes, Jesus got very tired and he needed to rest. Although he liked helping people, sometimes Jesus needed to be on his own. So then he would climb up a hill, or perhaps sail out in a little boat onto a lake, where the crowds would not follow him. Then Jesus would talk to God, his father, and he would have a rest. Jesus knew he could always talk to God about anything.

Jesus' friends knew that Jesus talked to God every day. 'Will you teach us to pray, please?' they asked him.

'Of course,' said Jesus. 'This is one way to do it. First of all, find somewhere quiet, then think about God. You don't need to talk out loud so that everybody can hear you. Just think about how special God is – like a king, like a very important person, or like a father who loves you very much. Then talk to him as if you were talking to your very, very best friend.'

'But what do we say to him?' the friends wanted to know.

'Ask God to help you always to do good things,' said Jesus, 'things that will make God and other people happy.'

'Then what?' asked the friends.

'Well,' answered Jesus, 'because God loves you, he cares about you. So ask him to give you food and everything else you need to keep you strong and healthy. And ask him to look after you so you are kept safe from danger.'

'Then what?' asked the friends.

'Say sorry for the things you have done or said which were unkind, and upset other people,' Jesus told them. 'God wants you and your friends to say sorry to each other when you've argued or hurt each other. God wants to forgive you, and always be your friend.'

Jesus' friends were pleased he had told them how to pray. Now they could talk to God too.

## Rhyme time

    2-3 mins

### Talking to God
*This rhyme expresses joys and fears in a childlike way. We can chat to God about anything!*

I want to say, 'Hello, God,'
And tell you about today.
I found lots of shells,
And saw some crabs
Scampering away.
I splashed in the sea,
And I jumped the waves,
Built castles out of sand,
And tried to count the grains,
Trickling through my hand.
I found slimy slugs on the path.
They gave my mum a fright.
But I don't like bad dreams
I sometimes have at night.
Thunderstorms scare me too,

And lightning in the sky.
I don't like crowded shops,
Or big lorries rumbling by.

So I want to ask you, God,
'Please look after me.'

## Song time

    5 mins

### Talk to God
*Explain that however we are feeling, whatever time it is and wherever we are, we can talk to God. God cares about us and he is always willing to listen to what we want to tell him. The tune is 'She'll be coming round the mountain'.*

When you're happy, really happy,
 talk to God, (repeat)
When you're feeling really happy,
 why not tell God all about it?
When you're happy, really happy,
 talk to God.

When you're frightened,
 very frightened…

When you're sad…

When you're sorry…

When you're worried…

In the daytime or the night-time…

## Pray time

   3-4 mins

### The Lord's Prayer
*Play some quiet instrumental music. Dim the room lights, and light a candle or nightlight. For safety, place it in a votive holder or jam jar where the children can easily see it but not touch it. Suggest that everyone listens quietly to the music, looks at the candle, and thinks about what a special person God is. Remind them that God loves and cares for each of them very much. Then suggest that they imagine God is sitting right next to them in the room and smiling at them. What would they like to tell him? Finish by reading the words of the Lord's Prayer, in a modern version or singing the Calypso version, from JU, p94.*

## Extra time

•Enjoy reading *The Lord's Prayer for Children* by Lois Rock, Lion or *My Little Prayer Box* by F Thatcher, SU.

•Look at material produced by Christian Aid, Tear Fund, or other relief agencies. Think about people who do not have enough to eat.

## Adults too

The Lord's Prayer is the one prayer that everyone used to learn at school or church. Older adults remember the traditional words, younger ones with some church background may know the more modern version. However, you cannot assume that everybody will have learned the prayer at school, particularly if yours is a multi-cultural, multi-faith area. Jesus used this prayer as a pattern: acknowledging the greatness and holiness of God; asking for his help in doing the right things; asking for protection from danger and to provide everything we need. Then, there's the element of saying sorry. The Lord's Prayer is a recognition that Christians are part of a worldwide family – we are praying to God together as 'our father', not just as 'my father'. Some people find difficulty praying to God as their father, especially if their relationship with their human father has been strained or non-existent. Others may find the idea of having such a personal relationship with God difficult. Encourage, but always be sensitive to individual needs.

## Top tip

Kathy says, 'Use glove puppets as a signal when you need quiet. Our friendly rabbit appears at prayer times, or during a devotional reading (for adults). Often a child holds him. We also have a monkey who hates noise. If the story is a quiet one and the children are boisterous, he puts his hands over his ears or hides behind the storyteller. This usually gets the message across without using words.'

**ACTIVITY PAGE:**
**The photocopiable activity page for this outline is on page 67**

Photocopy this page directly onto thin card, if possible.

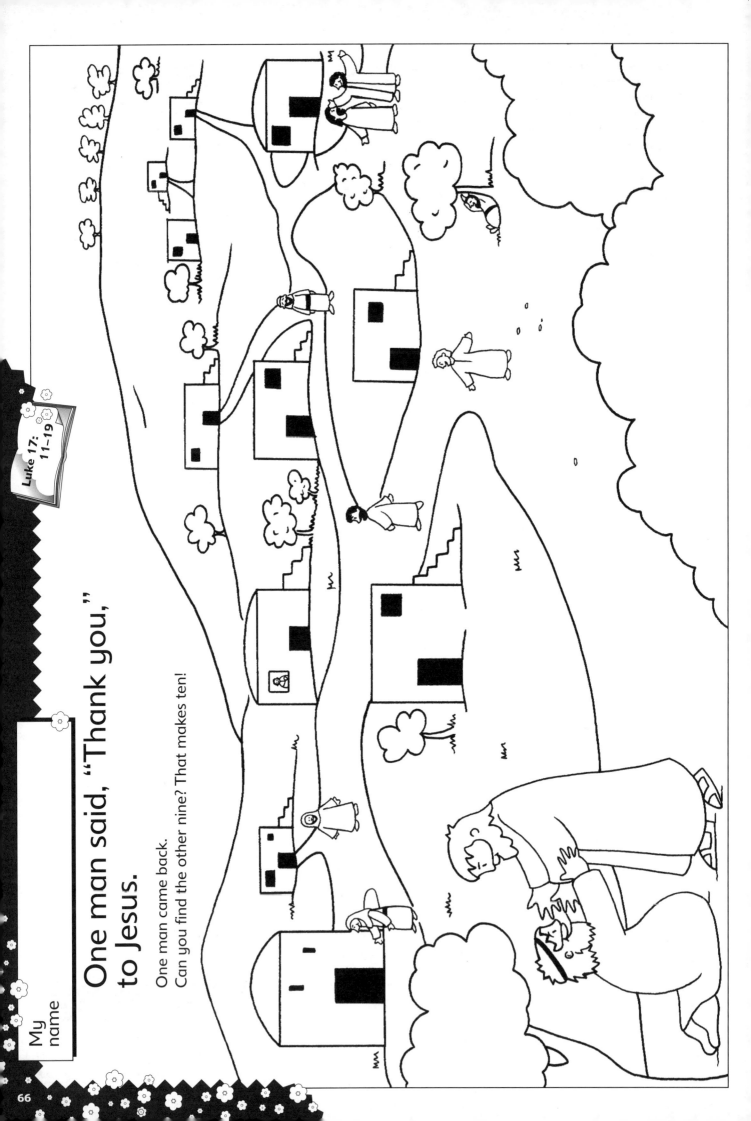

# One man said, "Thank you," to Jesus.

One man came back.
Can you find the other nine? That makes ten!

Luke 17: 11–19

My name

# I can talk to God.

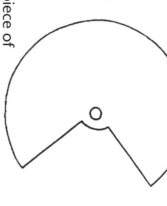

Matthew 6:5–14

Colour the pictures on the circle. Cut out the circle.

Cut a piece of card the same size and shape as the circle. Cut out a section like this.

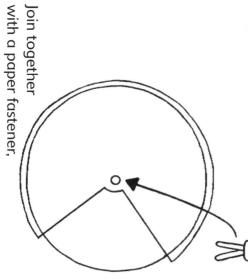

Join together with a paper fastener, like this.

Use this shape to make your own picture wheel about anything you wish.

## 19 Let's find out about Jesus
# Jesus the storyteller –
### The story of the sower

Luke 8: 4–8

## Play time

no limit

### Sand play

Theme your sand pit by adding an assortment of plastic plant pots, small spades, rakes and other plastic gardening tools, plus a few artificial flowers to 'plant' in the pots.

### Supermarket shopping

Set an area out as a shop with a checkout till at an accessible height. Include a display with empty packets of food items made from flour and cereal crops. You will also need toy money and shopping bags (be aware of safety issues if using plastic).

### Play dough

Use your favourite recipe to mould and shape. Or you might like to try this one:

### Jelly play dough

*1 cup flour*
*1/2 cup salt*
*1 cup water*
*1 tablespoon / 15 ml oil*
*2 teaspoons / 10 ml cream of tartar*
*1 packet gelatine*
*small quantity food colouring*

Mix all the ingredients together in a saucepan and cook over a medium heat, stirring constantly, until dough is the consistency of mashed potato. Leave to cool.

This can be used for pretend 'baking' activities if pastry and biscuit cutters, rolling pins and baking tins are provided. Alternatively, allow free play and the experience of feeling, prodding and moulding the dough. Do not allow the children to taste the dough as it is very salty.

### Bread rolls

*You will need: a packet of bread mix – many varieties are available in supermarkets, but be aware of allergy, hygiene and safety issues.*

Follow the directions on the packet. The dough can either be formed into a loaf or small rolls. If time is short, the latter are quicker. Ask a helper to be responsible for the cooking. Keep the children away from the hot areas. This is a directed activity which allows the children to discover how bread is made and what dough feels like, as well as one use of flour and seeds, and the smell and taste of fresh bread.

## Game time

5-10 mins

### What's inside?

*You will need: a variety of fruits, (eg pear, apple, peach, melon, tomato).*

Ask the children to guess how many seeds are inside each fruit. Use appropriate words (seed, stone, pip). One at a time, cut the fruit open and ask for help in counting the seeds to see which person has guessed most accurately. Explain that, with good soil, warmth and water, the tiny seeds could eventually grow into plants or trees that will produce more.

You could also devise a game using bean bags, eg catching or throwing into bucket or hoop targets.

## Making time

10-20 mins

### Bird headbands

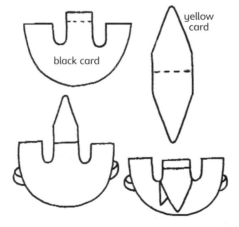

black card

yellow card

Give each child a headband, 2.5 cm deep, cut from coloured card. Staple or tape it to the size required. Add a bird's head shape, completed as shown, to the centre of the headband.

### Corn pictures

*You will need: for each child a piece of A4 card with a green line drawn on it to represent a stalk of corn; yellow card; pots of golden brown or yellow paint, mixed thickly; some small oval printing blocks to represent ears of corn.*

Show the children how to print the blocks in pairs on either side of the stalk. Give each child two leaf-shaped pieces of golden-yellow card, to represent the leaves. Glue in place, as shown.

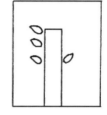

### Poppy field

For very young children, provide paints in harvest colours (yellow, golden brown) and some poppy shapes cut from red tissue paper, to collage on to the painted background.

## Story time

5-7 mins

### The sower

*You will need: a shoulder bag containing small pieces of brown tissue paper to represent seeds.*

Ask someone to walk around the room as you tell the story and scatter the 'seeds' as they go and mime to the story. You might like to say that this story is like one that Jesus told his friends.

Farmer Joe wanted to grow some corn. He hoped it would grow big and strong because he wanted to make it into flour – some to sell, and some to make into bread and cakes for himself and his family to eat.

So, he ploughed his field and began to sow the seed. He walked up and down the field, throwing the seeds from his bag as he walked.

Some of the seeds landed on the path. Some birds flew by and saw the seeds lying there. 'Delicious!' they chirped and they swooped down and gobbled it up. Oh dear, that seed wasn't going to grow into corn, was it?

The wind blew some of the seeds onto rocky ground at the edge of the field. The seeds started to grow, but the soil was too hard and dry. The plants did not have enough water for their roots to drink. The sun shone, and the little plants began to droop. Their leaves went dry and shrivelled, and the plants died. Farmer Joe wasn't very pleased. Those seeds weren't going to grow into corn either.

Some other seeds were blown into a patch of prickly weeds. Soon they sprouted and began to grow. But the weeds grew even quicker and soon they were enormous. The corn had no room to grow and so the little plants went yellow and died. Oh dear, what was Farmer Joe going to do?

But most of the corn seed fell onto the part of the field which had been ploughed. The soil there was good and there were no rocks or weeds. The rain watered the ground and the plants grew big and strong. The sun shone and turned the corn a golden brown colour ready for it to be harvested.

Farmer Joe cut the ripened corn, and ground the seeds into flour. He put it into sacks. He sold some of it at the market, and the rest was used to make bread and cakes for him and his family. And that made Farmer Joe a very happy man.

## Rhyme time

*Improvise actions as you chant this rhyme. Some children might like to wear bird headbands and peck up the seeds!*

These are the seeds the farmer sowed,
So that he would have lots of corn.

These are the seeds that fell on the path,
But the birds ate them up,
So the farmer had no corn. *(Shake head, look sad.)*

These are the seeds that
    fell near the rocks,
But the ground was too hard,
So the farmer had no corn.

These are the seeds that fell into thorns.
There was no room to grow,
So the farmer had no corn.

These are the seeds that fell on good soil,
The plants grew and grew, so
The farmer had lots of corn. *(Big smile.)*

## Song time

**The farmer sows the seed**
*Sing this song to the tune: 'The farmer's in his den'. Sing it through a couple of times, adding your own mimed actions as you go.*

The farmer sows the seed, *(repeat)*
Here, there, in his field,
The farmer sows the seed.

Some seeds fell on the path, *(repeat)*
Birds flew down, they gobbled up
The tasty seeds for lunch.

Some seeds fell near the rocks, *(repeat)*
The sun was hot, the small plants died,
The soil was much too hard.

Some seeds fell near the weeds, *(repeat)*
The small plants died, they could not grow,
The weeds were much too big.

Some seeds fell on good soil, *(repeat)*
They grew and grew, into lots of corn,
The farmer was so pleased!

## Pray time

**Good food**
*You will need: objects or pictures to represent the words in italics in the prayer; eg a packet of seeds, a toy tractor, a paper bag.*

*Make sure everyone is holding one of the objects. Ask the children to wave their object or picture in the air when they hear it mentioned. When the word 'food' is mentioned, all children holding a food item should respond. When 'everything' is mentioned, the whole group should respond. Practise this first and then lead the prayer.*

Thank you God, for *farmers* who grow food for us to eat.
Thank you for sending rain and sunshine to make *seeds* grow into strong plants.
Thank you for people who work in *bakeries* and *food factories*.
Thank you for all the people who work in *shops* and *supermarkets*.
And thank you for our families who make

sure we have enough food to eat.
For everything you give us, thank you, Father God.                Amen.

## Extra time

•Read *Stories Jesus Told*, Make and Learn series, SU. *Little Red Hen*, traditional; *The Little Seed* by Eric Carle, Puffin.

•Plant grass seed in polystyrene cups almost full of soil. Draw a face on the front of each cup. The seeds will, if watered, grow into 'hair'.

•Play with a toy farm.

## Adults too

The parables Jesus told could be enjoyed by everyone, whatever their age and understanding. They were stories related to everyday life. Children can enjoy exploring this theme at the level of seeds, plants, soil, growth, harvest and to discover where their food comes from. However, at a deeper, spiritual level this story is about ensuring conditions for growth. The way we care for the adults who come to groups with their under-fives is also vitally important. Providing a friendly welcome, support, time to listen, encouragement and understanding; accepting and loving them as people in their own right (rather than as someone's parent or guardian). These things help to build up relationships and trust and, when the opportunity arises, give us the opportunity to speak to them about the Christian faith.

## Top tip

Children learn through 'looking with their fingers'; a curiosity that wants to find out about things through touch as well as looking, or questioning. Encourage them to find out about soil, sand, and dough through 'hands-on' experiences. It's a fun way to discover about texture, but can also be used as an opportunity to develop language skills, eg think about words that describe uncooked dough: 'soft', 'squidgy', 'sticky'. Does it feel, look or smell the same when cooked?

**ACTIVITY PAGE:**
The photocopiable activity page for this outline is on page 72

# Jesus reads God's book

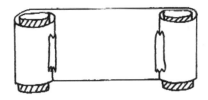

Luke 4: 16–30

## Play time

no limit

### Discovering wood

*You will need: wooden objects for children to look at and touch; splinter-free blocks of wood to sand; sandpaper; cloths and polish; plastic woodworking tools.*

Let the children explore the wooden objects. Walk around where you meet and ask them to think about which objects are made of wood. Show the children how to smooth the blocks of wood with sandpaper and apply polish (under careful supervision). The children could also play at being carpenters.

### Wood rubbings

*You will need: wax crayons and white paper to make rubbings of wooden objects, eg table, floorboards, or bark on trees.*

Allow the children to make their rubbings. Develop language skills by talking about the texture, colour and patterning of wood. Talk about the process of trees becoming furniture.

### Book corner

Make this a comfortable area with bean bags or soft cushions. Choose books about growing up and life experiences as well as some Bible stories about Jesus. With a few children, play 'spot the difference' by reading *If I had Lived in Jesus' Time* by P Graystone and J Thomas, SU. This book shows the differences in the environment in which Jesus grew up and the everyday life today's children (in Western countries) know.

Set out a craft table where children can make their own simple books: folding several sheets of paper in half, or stapling down one edge, or punching holes and tying pages with a ribbon. These could be scrapbooks or contain children's own artwork.

### Walkabout

With plenty of supervision, take the children on a walk around the community where you live. Look at the different kinds of buildings you pass: houses, shops, churches, schools, library, supermarkets. Do the children know any of the people who live or work in them?

## Game time

7-10 mins

### We went to church this morning...

Play a game based on the nursery favourite 'I went to school this morning and I walked like this…' Explain that you are going to play a game about going to church. The sort of activities you mime and the amount of explanation and discussion you need, will depend on the children's experiences. Include verses that show praying, singing, reading or hearing from the Bible, sitting, etc.

Set out some chairs in rows, add a table at the 'front' and some other props which will help the children imagine they are in a church building. Then chant or sing:

We went to church this morning and
    we sang like this,
Sang like this, sang like this,
We went to church this morning and
    we sang like this,
When we went to church.

Allow enough time to demonstrate what went on 'at church': you could sing a well-known worship song, or read a real Bible story to them from a children's Bible.

## Making time

5-15 mins

### Scrolls

*You will need: paper, glue, two cardboard rolls, ribbon, Bibles.*

Give each child a piece of parchment-coloured paper to draw or write on. Place a cardboard roll at each end, fold paper over, and glue to secure. Roll up the scroll from both ends and fasten with ribbon or thin cord. Show some different modern Bibles and perhaps a picture of an ancient scroll so that the children can compare them.

Explain that, when Jesus was a boy, books looked like this and were kept in the synagogue. People read aloud from them at the services, just like the Bible is read in churches today.

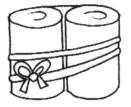

## Story time

4-5 mins

### Jesus reads God's book

*You will need: some props to tell the story – a hammer, plane, piece of wood, picture of someone reading from a large scroll, scroll made from parchment-coloured paper.*

*Enjoy the unusual word 'synagogue' and let the children join in with saying it, each time it occurs in the story.*

When he was a little boy, Jesus lived with his family in a village called Nazareth. His father, Joseph, was a carpenter. Joseph made chairs and tables and all the wooden things people needed for their homes. As Jesus grew older, he helped to make tables and chairs for other people too. Everybody in the village knew Jesus and his family.

On a special day each week, Jesus went to the synagogue – just like people go to church on Sundays. He liked to listen to the men reading from the big scrolls that were kept there. These scrolls were very special because they were about God. There was singing and prayers, and someone would speak, just like we have in our church services.

One day, when Jesus had grown up and become a man, he went to the synagogue in Nazareth where his family lived. This time, Jesus himself read aloud from God's book. He read about the special person whom God had promised to send to help the people of Israel. 'This person is going to do wonderful things,' he read. 'He will make ill people well again. He will help people who have no money. He will make blind people see. He will help people – everybody who is in trouble.' Jesus finished reading and fastened the scroll. Then he said, 'And today, that special person has arrived.'

The people in the synagogue were amazed.

'Yes, it's me,' said Jesus.

Everybody gasped. How could it be Jesus?

They had known Jesus since he was a little boy. They had watched him grow up. Joseph and Jesus had made lots of their furniture. They knew all about him because Jesus and his family lived in their small village. They had even heard all about the wonderful things Jesus had done in other towns, like making blind people see and making people who were ill, well again. 'But, nobody important ever came from Nazareth,' they said to each other.

But, this time, they were wrong! Jesus is the special person whom God sent!

## Rhyme time

2–6 mins

### Someone special

*Pretend to be the people listening to Jesus and thinking about who he might be.*

God's promised to send someone,
    somebody special,
Someone who will be a friend to the poor.
Will it be a king or a very rich person?
Who is it, we wonder? We're not sure.

God's promised to send someone,
    somebody special,
Someone who can make blind people see.
Will it be a doctor or a very clever person?
Who is it, we wonder? Who can it be?

God's promised to send someone,
    somebody special,
Someone who can help anyone in need.
What did you say? It's Jesus of Nazareth?
But we know him. That's a surprise indeed!

### Other rhymes
From *LACH*,
SU, 'I like books', p86,
'The library', p84

## Song time

5–7 mins

### All together!

*Choose verses from this song to suit your own group. The tune is 'We all clap hands together'. (Music can be found in* This little puffin…, *Elizabeth Matterson, Puffin Books.) As soon as you are familiar with the song, add mime or actions and improvise more verses to demonstrate things you do together.*

We go to church together,
We go to church together,
We go to church together,
As Jesus used to do.

We read God's book together…
As Jesus used to do.

We pray to God together …
As Jesus taught us to.

We all care for each other…
As Jesus wants us to.

We all praise God together…
As Jesus wants us to.

## Pray time

3–5 mins

### Jesus is special

*Pass a piece of smoothed wood around the group. Let everyone feel it and look at the patterns in it. Remind the children that Jesus learned from Joseph how to use tools to make pieces of wood into beautiful furniture. But that later he stopped working with wood and went around the country helping and healing people. He could do this because he was the special person God had promised to send. Pass the wood around the circle again. Suggest that each person completes the one line prayer, 'Jesus, you are special because…' If someone does not want to say anything, they can pass the wooden block to the next person. Finish by saying together, 'Jesus you are very special, and we praise you.'*

## Extra time

•Read *What's in the Bible?* by Stephanie King; 'God and Me' series, SU.

•Go into a church building and quietly look around. Let the children take turns in standing at the lectern to 'read' the Bible while the others listen.

•Look at pictures of a first century synagogue or temple and compare it with the church building you worship in or have seen.

•Role play being in a church service: give plenty of guidance to children who have not experienced going to church; observe those who are more used to it – and see what you learn about their understanding!

## Adults too

Jesus read Isaiah 61:1–2 aloud in the synagogue. What does it mean? How did/does Jesus free prisoners and captives, give sight to the blind and 'heal the broken-hearted'? Many people looking at the state of the world – and their own lives – will question Jesus' claims, as they did in his own home town. This outline may well trigger some of those doubts and questions for the parents and carers who have come along with the children. Try to give them the time and space to express their uncertainties: be prepared to discuss the issues and don't be too quick with an 'easy' Christian answer.

If there are adults in your group who express an interest in reading the Bible for themselves, the four titles of *Bread for the Journey* give an imaginative contemporary approach, looking at the question of identity: Who am I? Who is he? Who are we? Who are you? All available from your local Christian bookshop, Scripture Union mail order on 01908 856006 or www.scriptureunion.org.uk.

## Top tip

Pre-school children are not going to be able to get to grips with Isaiah! But *Tiddlywinks: My Little Books* will help them take their first steps in Bible reading. *My Little Green Book* uses the same Bible passages and themes as this book, with each page giving a short reading and an idea for talking to God. See page 89.

**ACTIVITY PAGE:**
The photocopiable activity page for this outline is on page 73

My name

# God helps the seeds to grow into plants.

Seeds and plants need warmth and water to grow big and strong. Colour the sun yellow, then draw some raindrops at the other side of your picture.

Use a green crayon and draw a new plant growing up from each seed.

How many birds are waiting to eat the seeds that fall on the path?

My name

# Jesus read from God's book.

Make your own scroll of the story. Colour in the pictures. Cut along the dotted line. Tape a rounded stick or narrow cardboard cylinder at each side. Roll up your scroll book.

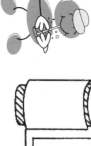

Luke 4: 16–30

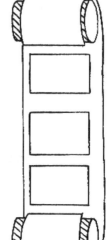

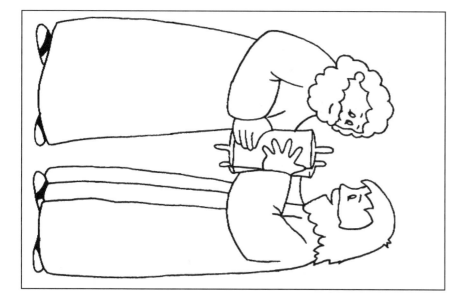

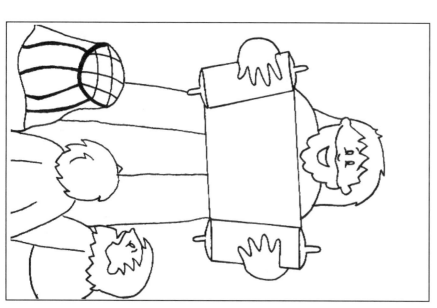

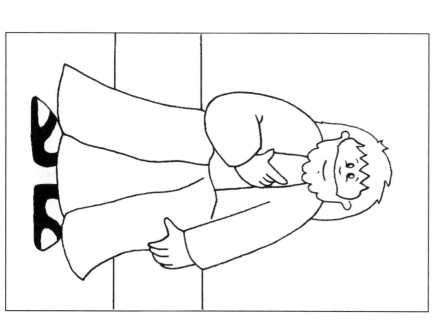

73

## 21 God knows when I'm feeling happy
# Jesus is alive and always with me

Matthew 28:1–10

## Play time

    no limit

### Best plays
*You will need: things to create a happy atmosphere – lively praise music playing; a cheerful environment created by a display of the children's work; using a brightly coloured tablecloth; having fresh flowers on the table (ensure that they are not poisonous).*

Have a variety of free play opportunities provided which the children enjoy. Include things you know they like doing and also one or more of these:

**Picnic play** – provide a small blanket, sun-hats, small towels, plastic crockery and cutlery and suitable containers in a basket for a 'picnic'. Other props could include an empty sunscreen container and plastic sunglasses. Teddies or dolls might also be invited on the 'picnic'!

Talk about feeling happy when we do things with our families and special friends.

**Transport play** – provide a transport mat or make one by drawing roads, fields, etc on a large sheet of card, which can be placed on the floor. Provide small plastic vehicles, small play people and small buildings (these can be made from packaging boxes) and other suitable props so that the children can create a mini-village. Encourage free play.

**Making pictures** – use sets of coloured shapes (gummed or cut from card) to create pictures. Encourage the children to tell you about the pictures which they have created. Make comments about 'feeling happy' when we can make something.

**Sand play** – provide a sand tray with damp sand and a variety of beach toys, eg plastic spades, buckets and moulds. Encourage children to explore building castles and making shapes with the moulds. Ask them if they have ever had holidays at the seaside and chat about the happy times they remember.

## Game time

 10-15 mins

### Happy game
Spread out around the room and then move 'along the road' using your whole body to express the words of the verse. Make up as many further happy verses as you like. Here are some to get you started…

Big happy teddy bears dancing along,
Dancing along, dancing along,
Big happy teddy bears dancing along,
Dancing along the road.

Happy wooden dollies marching along…

Lots of happy children skipping along…

Happy hoppy frogs jump-jumping along…

You can find music for this in *This Little Puffin*, E Matterson, Puffin, as 'Big floppy scarecrows dangling along'.

### Bean bags
Stand together in a circle. (If you have more than ten children, split into more than one group for this game.) A child tosses a brightly coloured bean bag to another child in the ring. Each child completes the statement, 'I feel happy when…' before throwing it to the next child.

## Making time

 20 mins

### Happy collage
*You will need: paper, glue; scissors; a tray of bright collage materials, eg coloured paper or fabric, ribbon, yellow paper circles.*

Encourage the children to glue pieces to a background to create a 'happy collage'.

### Happy cards
*You will need: approximately A5 size folded cards and brightly coloured broad felt-tipped pens.*

Encourage the children to draw their own 'happy' pictures on the front. Write a message on the inside if the child wishes you to do so.

### Praise ribbons
*You will need: large wooden or plastic curtain rings (about 8 cm diameter) and lengths of bright ribbon, (about 40 cm long).*

Create 'praise ribbons'. See diagram. Use these for free expression to lively praise music.

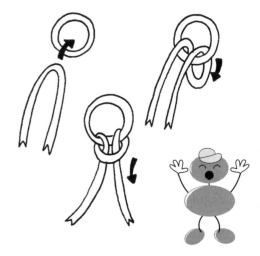

## Story time

 10-15 mins

### My Jesus is alive!
*You will need: small figurines to represent Mary and two friends, an angel and Jesus – these could be Duplo figures or play people, suitably dressed in scraps of fabric, or knitted finger puppets; garden materials – a sand tray, twigs for 'trees', pebbles, small flowers or plants and a small hollow cylinder; illustrated Bible.*

*Keep the figures out of sight until the appropriate point of the story. Involve children in creating a 'garden' from the materials provided. Explain that long ago, when somebody died, the people put the dead person in a special grave like a cave, called a tomb. As you talk, let children place the 'tomb' in the garden. (This could be covered with moss). Create a path leading to the tomb. Explain that when Jesus died, his friends put his body inside the tomb. Put a large stone in front of the 'tomb'. Continue with the story.*

Mary felt so sad. Her friend Jesus had died. Mary and her friends were going to his tomb. *('Walk' Mary and friends along the path, towards the tomb.)* They talked about their special friend Jesus.

'He was always so kind. He was my best friend.'

Suddenly the ground shook. There was an angel! *(Move the stone to one side. Stand angel beside the 'tomb'.)*

'Don't be afraid. Jesus is not dead. Look! His body is not here. He is alive! Go and tell his friends.'

Mary was so excited. She couldn't believe it. 'My Jesus is alive!' She was so happy. She clapped her hands. She started running. She wanted to tell her friends.

Running! Running! 'My Jesus is alive!' *('Run' figures back down the path.)*

Then suddenly – stop! *(Stop figures. Place 'Jesus' in front of them.)* Someone was standing there! Do you know who it was? It was Jesus! Standing right there!

'Hello!' said Jesus.

Mary couldn't believe it. 'My Jesus is alive!' Jesus was talking to her! Mary was so happy she fell down. She hugged Jesus' feet. 'My Jesus is alive!'

*Have an illustrated Bible ready at this passage. Show the children the Bible passage. Explain that this is not a made-up story. It is in the Bible because it is true. It really happened. Tell them that Mary was so happy because Jesus was alive again. Explain that you are happy too, because you know that Jesus is alive.*

## Rhyme time

### Poor Mary, happy Mary
*Say this rhyme with actions or sing it to the tune of 'Poor Jenny is a-weeping'.*

Mary is a-weeping, a-weeping, a-weeping. *(Cry.)*
Mary is a-weeping. Her Jesus is dead. *(Shake head.)*

She's walking to the tomb now, tomb now, tomb now. *(Make 'tomb' with thumb and finger of left hand, 'walk' two fingers down left arm.)*
She's walking to the tomb now. Her Jesus is dead. *(Shake head.)*

The angel is waiting, waiting, waiting, *(Fluttering both hands, then hold first finger upright and still.)*
The angel is waiting! My Jesus is alive! *(Smile! Clap hands on 'Jesus' and then point both first fingers upwards!)*

Mary is so happy, so happy, so happy, *(BIG smiles.)*
Mary is so happy. My Jesus is alive! *(BIG smiles.)*

## Song time

### I am happy
*Enjoy singing this happy song to the tune of 'The wheels on the bus'. Encourage the children to make appropriate actions.*

I smile and sing when I feel happy, I feel happy, I feel happy,
I smile and sing when I feel happy.
I feel warm inside!

I shout and clap when I feel happy, ...
I feel warm inside!

*Chat about how good it feels when we are happy and excited. Ask children to say what makes them feel excited. Sing verse two again. Then say 'we go to bed feeling happy and warm inside when we've had a lovely day. Let's pretend we're sleepy and going to bed now.' Repeat first verse slowly to calm children before your next activity.*

## Pray time

### Happy times
*If possible, arrange with parents and carers to provide a photograph of their child with family on a recent holiday or day's outing. Let each child chat about their photo. Then pray short 'thank you' prayers for each child's holiday. Either the children themselves could pray, if they are confident, or the leader could do so, eg 'Dear Jesus, thank you for the happy time Susan had on her picnic.'*

*Alternatively, provide pictures from magazines or from colouring books of children enjoying typical activities and use these for discussion and prayer. If there are more than ten children in the group split into two smaller groups for this activity. Remember to say thank you for the happy time you're having today too!*

## Extra time

• Read *God Knows,* Little Fish book, SU.

• Create a praise poster, using Psalm 100:1 as inspiration. Guide the children to make handprints to decorate the poster.

• *Really, Really Excited* by Leena Lane, SU, is one of the 'God and Me' series of little books from Scripture Union, exploring children's emotions.

## Adults too

Children do not automatically have a vocabulary to describe their feelings. Helping them to develop an awareness of their feelings helps them to develop a better understanding of themselves and of others. For example, you might say, 'You feel happy when you see the bubbles floating up into the air,' or 'You are feeling excited about the picnic.' Talking in this way may seem artificial at first but it gives children the words to define the vague, and sometimes confusing, feelings that they are experiencing. Suggest that adults buy a small cheerful jotter pad and record times that they noticed when their children were happy and how they helped their children gain awareness of their emotions with this type of simple comment.

Use the pad too, to record 'Today I felt happy when …' or to think of one thing each day that they felt thankful to God for. (When we are feeling depressed or 'a bit low', learning to focus on the positive things in our lives can help us to gradually move to a happier outlook.)

## Top tip

Create a 'happy board' for your meeting room. Pin up inspiring quotations, beautiful pictures, cartoons, 'good news' stories. Encourage adults to contribute to the board. Regularly update it and ensure it looks attractive and uncluttered to maintain interest. A board with both a pinboard section and a whiteboard (with marker pens available) can encourage spontaneous 'thoughts for the day'. Real sayings from children can be a fun addition.

**ACTIVITY PAGE:**
The photocopiable activity page for this outline is on page 78

# The unforgiving servant

Matthew 18:21–35

## Play time

no limit

### Fuzzy felt

*You will need: 'fuzzy felt boards' or make your own by securing soft flannelette over small boards; a variety of pre-cut felt shapes – blank faces (different colour skins), eyes, happy/sad/angry mouths, noses, hair, hats and ribbons.*

Encourage children to create their own faces on the fuzzy felt board. Chat about the 'people' they create and how the 'people' are feeling. Let the child express their own thoughts: adults need to be careful not to impose their ideas!

### Play dough

Provide generous quantities of play dough. Ensure the consistency is satisfying to work with (too sticky or too dry can be very frustrating). Play some tumultuous music that conveys anger (eg some of the songs from *Les Miserables* but be careful what you choose!) Encourage the children to listen to the music and to show how the music feels by using the play dough.

### Building blocks

Encourage children to see how high a tower they can build before it falls down. Ensure that the space is safe and that falling blocks will not cause damage or injury. To avoid accidents, do not let the children build higher than they can reach from the floor, ie, they may not stand on a chair to build higher.

### Grumpy bear

Enlarge the picture of Grumpy bear. Give each child a copy to hold or put a large version on the wall. With a few children at a time ask, 'Why is Grumpy bear looking so cross?' and then 'What makes you feel cross sometimes?'

## Game time

8-10 mins

### Feelings cards

*You will need: pairs of card circles (about 15 cm in diameter). With a black marker pen, draw different facial expressions on each pair.*

Encourage children to find 'two the same'. Chat about the feelings in the pictures.

### Cross pebbles

*You will need: a transparent plastic bowl (a small fish bowl works well), deep tray, water coloured with blue food colouring, pebbles.*

Place the container on a large, deep baking tray (to catch the water). Pour in the light blue water until the bowl is filled to the brim. Suggest that the water makes us think of all the happy things in our lives. Ask the children to think of things that make them cross. As a child tells you something that makes them cross, they place a pebble in the water.

When the water is displaced, show the children that the water has gone out. There isn't room for the water if it is full of stones. If we are full of cross things, there isn't room for happy things!

## Making time

15-20 mins

### Cross paintings

*You will need: large sheets of paper, red, black and purple paint, and broad brushes (about 10 cm breadth).*

Talk about how we feel inside when we are feeling angry. Ask children to use the colours to show how they feel inside when they are angry.

### Cross faces

*You will need: small mirrors.*

Encourage the children to make cross faces. Older children will enjoy trying to draw a cross face, using broad wax crayons: encourage observation in the mirror.

## Story time

10 mins

### The unforgiving servant

*You will need: play money; a puppet; three play figures to represent the characters in the story; a small, clean hamster or bird cage to represent the jail, or glue paper strips to form bars on the front of a shoebox. Or present the story as a puppet show, with three hand puppets and loud narration.*

*To help children understand the story, begin with a puppet asking you for some money. Say, 'Yes, you can borrow some money from me but you must pay it back.' Puppet agrees and borrows money.*

*Puppet says, 'I owe you some money. I will pay it back soon.' (Exit puppet.)*

*Ask the children how much money the puppet owes you. Then bring the puppet back, saying, 'Thank you for letting me use the money. Here is the money I owe you.' Thank puppet for paying you back. Move on to telling the Bible story about an angry man.*

Once upon a time there lived a man who owed a lot of money to the king. (Seat king on throne. Bring other man in front of him.)

'Where is my money?' asked the king.

'I'm sorry. I don't have it,' said the man. 'I will try to save some money and pay it back to you.'

The king was a good man. 'That's all right,' he said. 'You don't have to pay back the money, I will forgive you.'

The man was glad. He walked outside. He was glad the king said it was all right. ('Walk' man away from king.)

Then he saw a man who owed him a little bit of money. (Bring second man up to first.)

'Give me my money,' he said in a cross voice.

'I'm sorry. I don't have it,' said the second man. 'I will try to save some money and pay it back to you.'

'Give me my money – now!' shouted the first man in a very cross voice.

'Please forgive me. I will pay your money back to you,' promised the second man.

'No! No! No!' shouted the angry man. 'I'm going to put you in jail!' *(Put 'second man' in 'jail'.)*

Some people ran and told the king what had happened. The king was very cross. 'I forgave you,' he said. 'But you didn't forgive somebody else. Now you must go to jail!' *(Put 'first man' in jail.)*

## Rhyme time

### Feeling cross

*Share the rhyme, then ask the children if they ever feel like that. What do they do to make the angry feelings go away?*

Sometimes I feel sort of cross,
I want my mum to think I'm boss.
I stomp about and moan a lot.
My face and cheeks feel kind-of hot.

Then I bash the play dough,
Or punch and punch and punch my
    pillow.
The angry feeling goes away.
Then I feel like I can play.

## Song time

### Angry feelings

*Introduce this song about feelings which goes to the tune of 'What shall we do with the drunken sailor?' Use suggestions made by the children to create other verses. If a child suggests a negative outlet (eg 'I smack my sister') talk about this: how do we think our sister feels? What will happen if we do this? Gently encourage children to be aware of how our actions affect others and how there are consequences to our actions.*

What shall I do with my angry feelings,
What shall I do with my angry feelings,
What shall I do with my angry feelings,
When I get all cross inside?

Find someone who I can talk to…

Punch my pillow or a cushion…

*End Song time by asking children to think of somewhere they feel nice and safe. Assure them that Jesus loves each one of us and he understands how we feel, even when we're feeling angry.*

## Pray time

### Feeling angry

*You will need: paper, crayons.*

*Ask children to draw a picture showing how they feel when they are angry. Tell them that Jesus understands when we feel angry and we can talk to him about everything. Use this prayer with individual children or with the whole group.*

Dear Jesus,
Thank you that you understand when I feel angry, when I feel like I want to shout and scream and even hurt somebody. Please help mummy and daddy *(adapt as appropriate)* to listen to me so that I can tell them how I'm feeling and we can talk about what's making me feel cross. Amen.

*Tell children that if they want to, they can tear up their angry pictures into little pieces. (Provide a bin for the scraps.)*

## Extra time

•Read *I'm sorry*, Little Fish book, SU.

•'Sometimes I smack when I'm angry' *LACH*, p82.

•Angry song – create verses for 'The wheels on the bus' about feeling angry.

•Dressing up: provide props and a suitable area for a 'prison' for the children to enact the Bible story.

## Adults too

Here's a modern parable that you can tell to both adults and children. Tell the story enthusiastically, with plenty of miming actions, to hold attention of both adults and children. This is how to catch a monkey.

Take a handful of grapes – make sure the monkey is watching you. Find a very small hole in a tree and put the grapes inside. Monkeys love grapes. Soon he will come down and put his hand in the hole. But when he holds the grapes his hand will be too big to get out of the hole. Monkeys love grapes so much that he won't let go – so he will be stuck in the tree! And then you can catch your monkey!

Children will enjoy the story at face value. For adults, explain how this story has the same message as today's Bible story. When we hold onto our 'grapes' of anger and unforgiveness, we remain trapped in one place. We need to ask ourselves, is there someone in our lives whom we need to forgive? Maybe we need to forgive ourselves too!

## Top tip

Consider: it has been said that the greatest lifetime threat to your child is anger! We have a responsibility to teach our children to handle their anger in effective ways, just as we train them to ride a bicycle. (We don't take the bicycle away because they wobble and fall off when they start!) When we suppress anger, it goes underground, leading to greater problems later on. Read more about this in *Kids in Danger* by Ross Campbell, Christian Art Publishers.

**ACTIVITY PAGE:**
The photocopiable activity page for this outline is on page 79

My name

# I feel happy when...

Talk about: why are these children feeling happy? What makes you feel happy?

Matthew
28:1–10

78

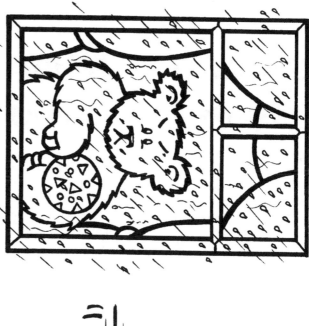

## God knows when I'm feeling cross.

Matthew
18:21–35

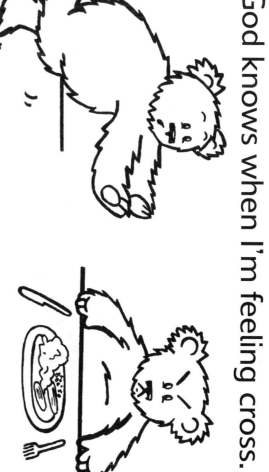

Talk about Grumpy Bear's
bad morning. What goes
wrong for Grumpy Bear?
How does he feel? Do things
go wrong for you sometimes?
How do you feel?

# 23 God knows when I'm feeling sad

# Nehemiah is sad

Nehemiah 1–3

## Play time

### Feelings game
*You will need: a simple game board, prepared with about thirty sections from start to finish. Every few 'spaces' draw a simple face with a different expression.*

Children shake dice and move a counter along the board. Each time they land on a 'face' they are encouraged to say, 'I feel sad/happy/angry when…'

### Block play
*You will need: wooden building blocks or other building sets, such as Duplo.*

Encourage house building, as a feature of today's Bible story.

### Sorting
*You will need: several shallow trays for sorting and a selection of safe natural objects (shells are ideal, but stones or leaves would also be suitable).*

Encourage children to sort the objects. Do not impose your ideas of how they should be sorted but rather encourage the children to explain their groupings. When discussing the activity, chat about how our feelings sometimes seem muddled up and it is good to be quiet so we can sort things out in our heads when we don't know what to do.

### Playhouse
*You will need: a very large box (eg, from an electrical appliance such as a washing machine) with one side cut off and a 'window' cut in the side; glue and squares of brightly coloured paper (about 8 cm square).*

Encourage the children to decorate the box. Suggest they might like to position the squares in rows like bricks. Have the box available within the room for children to explore inside and find a 'safe' place when they wish to. (Make sure you can see inside so you can supervise any play activity discreetly.)

## Game time

### Sardines
In a large room, create areas where children can hide. One child hides while the others shut their eyes. Children hunt for the hidden child. When a child finds the hidden child, they also squeeze into the hiding place. The children all squeeze into the hiding place as they discover it! (Call 'time' if the 'hiding' group becomes uncomfortably large!) Chat about how good it is to be all together!

## Making time

### Feeling 'blue'?
*You will need: several cold colours of paint (shades of blue, white, pale green), large sheets of grey paper (printed newsprint will do) and broad brushes; play sad, tranquil music, eg, Beethoven's Moonlight Sonata.*

Encourage the children to paint how the music makes them feel. This need not be a 'picture' – the child may choose to create lines, patterns, abstract shapes.

### Umbrella pictures

*You will need: a large sheet of newsprint for the background paper; outline shapes*

of open umbrellas drawn on pieces of various brightly coloured gift wrap; crayons or pens.

The children cut out the umbrellas and stick onto newspaper, then draw in umbrella handles. When all umbrellas are stuck on, use pale blue pastel to fill the page with raindrops. As children are working, chat about how even when things seem grey and sad, there are still bright, happy things around us and eventually the sun will shine again.

## Story time

### Nehemiah is sad
*You will need: a plastic goblet wrapped in foil to be a silver goblet on a tray. Prepare a scroll for the king's letter: colour-wash paper with cold tea to create an aged effect.*

Once a long, long time ago there lived a man named Nehemiah. That's a long name – can you say it? Nee – hu – my – ah.

Nehemiah's friends came to see him. He was happy to see his friends. But his friends told him some sad news: 'The walls of our big town, the city Jerusalem, are all broken down.'

Nehemiah was very sad to think that the walls were broken. *(Look sad.)*

Even after his friends left Nehemiah kept feeling sad.

Now Nehemiah worked for the king. His job was to take the king his special cup. *(Show silver goblet.)* The king looked at Nehemiah.

'Nehemiah, why are you looking so sad?' asked the king.

'The walls of my city are broken down,' sighed Nehemiah. 'There is nobody to fix them. Could I go to fix the walls of my city?'

'Yes,' said the king. And he gave Nehemiah a letter to tell the other leaders to help him. *(Show scroll.)*

When Nehemiah got to Jerusalem he saw that all the walls around the city were broken down. The gates were broken too.

Nehemiah talked to his people. 'We will fix the walls. God will help us do it,' he said. Now Nehemiah wasn't sad any more. He knew he had a big job to do. All the people had to work very hard. Some people laughed at them and thought they were silly to try to fix the walls. But Nehemiah said, 'We will fix the walls. God will help us do it.'

Some people said they would fight them if they fixed the walls. But Nehemiah said, 'We will fix the walls. God will help us do it.'

They worked and worked. They worked some more. After a long, long time they finished the big job. And Nehemiah said, 'We have fixed the walls. God helped us do it.'

Nehemiah was happy now. He had done the big job God wanted him to do.

## Rhyme time

### Sad eyes

*Chant this little rhyme, using a sad expression and voice. Don't be too authentic, or you will distress the children.*

My eyes start to cry when I'm sad,
My eyes start to cry when I'm sad,
My eyes start to cry and my lips
    start to tremble,
My eyes start to cry when I'm sad.

*Talk about what makes us feel sad. What can we do that makes us feel better?*

*Tell the children that Nehemiah prayed to God when he didn't know what he should do. God is always listening when we talk to him and he will help us, just like he helped Nehemiah.*

## Song time

### City walls

*The rhyme takes the rhythm of 'London Bridge is Falling Down'. Add actions to help the children feel a part of the story. Find a longer version of this song in* LSS, *p45.*

City walls are broken down, broken down, broken down, *(Walk sadly in circle, shaking heads.)*
City walls are broken down, *(Stop – hands above head and bring down.)*
Build them, Nehemiah. *(Wag finger, clap rhythm on his name.)*

Build strong walls and city gates, city gates, city gates, *(Walk in circle, with a springy step.)*
Build strong walls and city gates, *(Build fist over fist, or mime digging and building.)*
Build them Nehemiah. *(Wag finger, clap rhythm on his name.)*

Don't worry when people laugh, people laugh, people laugh, *(Walk in circle, wagging finger.)*
Don't worry when people laugh, *(Hands above heads.)*
Build them Nehemiah. *(Wag finger, clap rhythm on his name.)*

Build strong walls and city gates, city gates, city gates…

The walls and gates are strong again, strong again, strong again, *(Stand still and firm, with elbows bent and fists clenched.)*
The walls and gates are strong again – well done, Nehemiah!

## Pray time

### Feeling sad

*Look at your umbrella pictures together; or bring a photograph of a rainy scene. Ask the children, 'Does the rain just keep on and on raining or does it stop in the end?' Chat about how we sometimes feel sad, but that it does stop in the end.*

*Pray a short prayer based on this one:*

Thank you God that you understood when Nehemiah felt sad and you helped him to fix the walls.

Thank you that you understand when we feel sad. Help us to remember to talk to you about it. Please show us what we can do so that we feel better too.

*You could also use 'Who cares?' from* LACH, *p83.*

*Note: it's important that children don't feel it is 'wrong' to feel sad.*

## Extra time

•Bean bag blues. Seat children in a circle. Hold a drab beanbag and say 'I feel sad when ..' pass or throw the beanbag to any child. The child catches it and says 'I feel sad when …', then throws it to another

child. Repeat with the brightly coloured beanbag, this time saying, 'I feel better when …'

•*I Miss You* by Leena Lane is one of the 'God and Me' series of little books from Scripture Union, exploring children's emotions.

## Adults too

The 'PACER' (Parent and Child Enriched Relationships) parenting programme in West Cork, Ireland encourages parents to nurture the child's emotional development. One of the PACER tools is 'Name, claim and tame' – (these could be presented on three flashcards).

Sometimes we deny our children's negative feelings by distracting, maybe tickling the child, saying 'give me a smile', or giving a biscuit when the child is sad. However, we learn to accept our emotions by being able to name and claim them: 'my feelings are part of me – they are not wrong. It's what I do with them that counts!' Young children do not automatically have the vocabulary to understand and describe their feelings. We help them to claim their feelings and to tame them (to be in control of them) when we help them to name them. So we might say; 'I know you're feeling sad because your rabbit died…'

The book of Psalms is deeply expressive of a whole range of feelings. Have a look at one or two and see the honestly expressed feelings of the writers.

## Top tip

Don't ignore feelings. For example, when two children have a tussle over a toy, we tend to focus on sharing and making up. However, we will help our children if we acknowledge their feelings in tense moments, eg 'I know you're feeling angry and you want to hit Sam – but people are not for hurting. You can punch this cushion if you want.' Acknowledge the feeling and provide an acceptable outlet for the expression of that feeling.

**ACTIVITY PAGE:**
**The photocopiable activity page for this outline is on page 84**

# Gideon is afraid

Judges 6–8

## Play time

no limit

Themed play for this session is designed to set up situations where conversations about being shy or scared may arise, while giving the children an assurance of safety and care. Aim to strike a balance in assuring the children of God's power and protection, yet not frightening them or 'putting ideas in their heads'.

### Absorbing water
*You will need: an area where a spill won't matter; plastic droppers; a plastic container of water and various types of material, eg cotton, cotton wool, sponge, piece of foil (covering a piece of cardboard), piece of stiff plastic, tissue, kitchen paper, piece of varnished wood, metal lid, roof tile, etc.*

This play activity helps children to realise that we are safe in our homes because they are built of materials that do not absorb water.

Encourage the children to sort objects into which absorb water and which don't. Older children will enjoy predicting which category items will fall into before testing. Discuss and allow the children to discover what happens when we drop water onto different substances. Introduce the word, 'absorb'. Chat about what would happen if our raincoats were made of paper? What are our houses made of? Why? Explore how we may feel a bit scared in a rainstorm, but can know that we are safe in our houses because they are built to keep the rain out. (An example like a storm is impersonal and the children can think about it more objectively than, for instance, a fear of animals.)

### People who help us
*You will need: 'play people', toy vehicles and other suitable props for children to role play fire fighters, ambulances, rescue helicopters, trains, tractors and other items related to 'people who help us'.*

Give children enough free play time to explore different roles. Chat about feeling scared if there was danger or if we are hurt. Explain that God gives us people to help us.

## Game time

8-15 mins

### Pick-up sticks
*You will need: flat craft sticks dyed red, yellow, green, and blue, using food colouring.*

Ask 'How does this colour make you feel?' (Usually, yellow – happy, red – angry, blue – sad/scared, green – jealous, but listen to and acknowledge the child's interpretation.) Start the game by letting the sticks fall into a loose pile. Each child takes a turn to pick up a stick. If another stick moves, that turn is over. The child says the colour of their last stick, and talks about the feeling associated with that colour, eg 'I feel happy when I play with my cars.'

## Making time

15 mins

### Musical shakers
*You will need: paper plates, decorations, stapler, tape, dried beans, crêpe paper.*

Each child decorates the underneath of a pair of paper plates. Place a few dry beans between the plates and staple the two edges together (decorated sides facing outwards) to form a shaker. Tape over the ends of the staples. Alternatively, decorate cardboard tubes and firmly tape paper over both ends, after putting a few beans inside. Add short ribbons of crêpe paper to one edge for decoration. Use these shakers to make a 'rainstorm'.

### Rainstorm
Enlarge the set of pictures below. Show the pictures in order and involve children in explaining the story. Ask them if they can use their musical instruments to tell the story, as you show the pictures. Use shakers for rain and supply cymbals or saucepan lids for a thunderstorm.

Chat about how we can feel scared when it rains hard – but we are safe in our houses and the storm will go away.

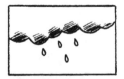

## Story time

15 mins

### Gideon feels scared
*You will need: a candle for each child (a real one unlit or a small cardboard tube with a crêpe paper flame in one end) and a 'trumpet' (made with long cardboard roll); a carpet in one corner of the room to be the 'camp'.*

Do you feel scared sometimes? Long ago there was a man called Gideon. He felt very scared. So did his family. And all their friends. Bad people kept coming and taking all their food and chasing them out of their houses. Gideon was so scared that he was hiding away in a cave. But one day God had a special job for him to do.

'Gideon, I want you and your people to chase these bad men away.'

'I can't do it,' said Gideon, 'I'm not big and strong. Nobody will listen to me.'

But God said, 'I will make you strong.' Gideon listened to God, even though he felt scared. He called his friends together and they made a secret plan.

At night time they sneaked up very quietly on the bad people, until they were all around them. *(At this point have children get up quietly and give each one a candle and a trumpet and get them to quietly stand around the perimeter of the carpet.)*

Gideon said, 'We will give them a big fright. Wait until I blow my trumpet. Then you must all blow your trumpets, show your bright lights and shout 'For God and for Gideon!' *(Help children to act this out. You will probably have to repeat it several times!)*

The bad people got such a big fright that they started running away.

All Gideon's people asked him to be their leader.

'No,' said Gideon. 'I am not your leader. God is our leader. He helped us when we were frightened. He helped us to be brave. He helped us make a clever plan! God helped us so that we could give the bad people a big fright and make them run away.'

God helped Gideon to chase the bad people away! Now Gideon did not need to be scared of them any more. God helped Gideon when he was scared. He helped him to be brave.

God wants to help us too. He will help us to do brave things – even when we feel scared.

## Rhyme time

**Gideon**
*Retell the story of Gideon with this rhyme.*

Gideon was a little man,
He wasn't big or brave.
The bad men came and he was scared.
He hid in a deep, dark cave.
'Come out, Gideon,' God said to him,
'Come – I'll make you strong.
We'll chase these bad men out you'll see.
I promise it won't take long.'
'Blow on your trumpets, loud,' said God.
'Blow on your trumpets – one, two, three!'

The trumpets blew,
    the lights shone bright.
The bad men didn't even try to fight.
'Run!' they shouted, 'Run for your life!'
Gideon's the winner with God on his side!

## Song time

**Baa baa brave sheep**
*Chat about feeling scared. Explain that feeling a bit scared is important: we would run in front of cars or we wouldn't remember to lock our house door to keep us safe if we didn't feel a bit scared. Even animals and grown ups feel scared sometimes but we can ask Jesus to keep us safe. This is a song about a sheep who knows he is safe because Jesus is looking after him. (Explain that 'fear' means 'scared' and that 'slumber' means sleep.)*

'Baa, baa brave sheep,
Have you any fear?'
'No sir, no sir, God is near.'
Jesus is the shepherd who
    watches the sheep,
He never slumbers and he never sleeps.
'Baa, baa brave sheep,
Have you any fear?'
'No sir, no sir, God is near.'

## Pray time

**I feel scared**
*Seat children in a circle and hold one end of a ball of pale blue or white wool. Say, 'I feel scared when …' and then ask children to pray with you, 'Thank you Lord that you look after us when we feel scared.' Then pass the ball of wool to a child, who says, 'I feel scared when …' The group thank you prayer is repeated each time. The child then keeps holding the strand of wool but passes the rest of the ball to another child. Gradually you will all link together. Pray:*

Lord Jesus,
Sometimes I feel scared like a little sheep who needs a shepherd to look after him. Please help me to remember that you love me and you are always looking after me. Thank you that I can always talk to you, even when I'm feeling scared.        Amen.

## Extra time

*Really, Really Scared* by Leena Lane is one of the 'God and Me' series of little books from Scripture Union, exploring children's emotions.

From *LACH*, 'Who cares?' p83; 'God is there' p81.

## Adults too

Helping children handle their emotions is not easy: it's not something we tend to feel comfortable about for ourselves, let alone for others. Explain that pretending that we don't feel something doesn't make the feeling go away. Rather our feelings are a sign that something needs attention – rather like a warning light flashing on the dashboard of the car. Suggest that it can be helpful to encourage family members to each have a 'feelings box', which each person can decorate for himself or herself. Younger children might have crayons, paper and play dough, a 'punching pillow' or favourite comfort toy in their boxes. Coloured pencils and pens and a journal might be helpful for older children and adults. Chat about other items that might be helpful to get in touch with your 'self', eg a CD with relaxing music, anti-stress face mask sachets, an aromatic candle, a few little cards with favourite Bible verses printed on them, a book of favourite poems or reflections.

## Top tip

Helping children to understand their emotions and to have empathy for others is an aspect of child nurturing in which not many of us have been trained. Understanding our emotions is almost like finding a piece of the jigsaw linking our spiritual growth with the physical world in which we live. A book which takes this idea further is *The Five Love Languages of Children* by Gary Chapman and Ross Campbell, Northfield Publishing.

**ACTIVITY PAGE:**
The photocopiable activity page for this outline is on page 85

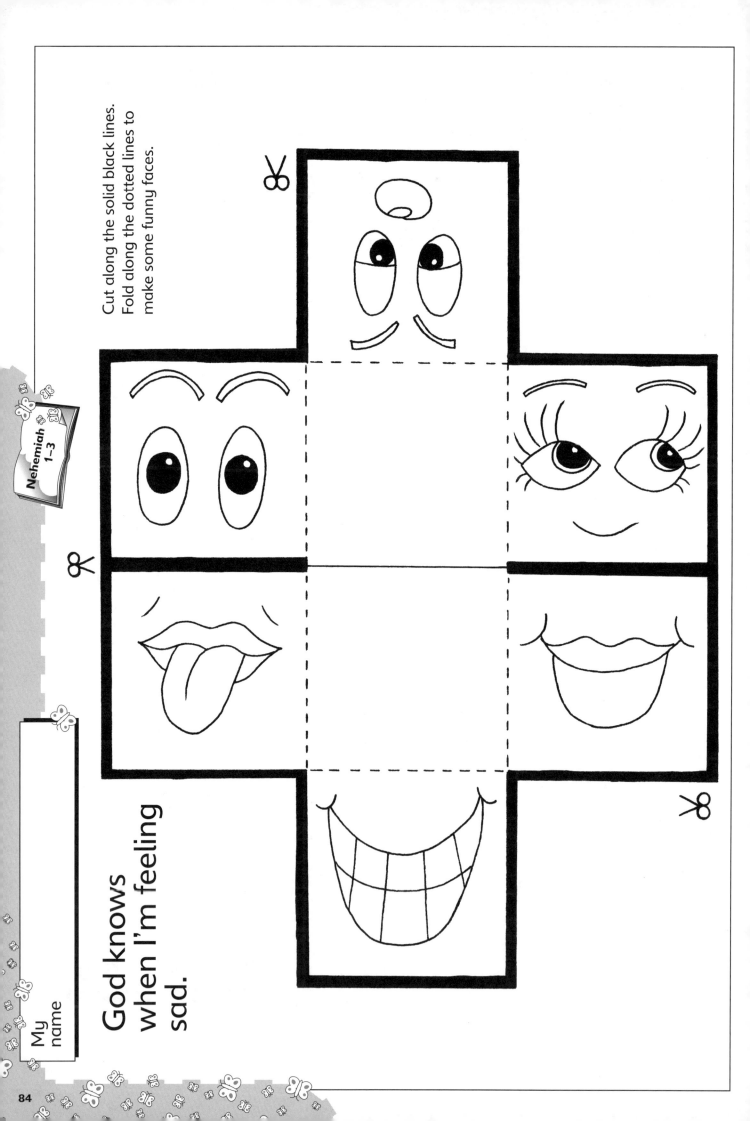

Cut along the solid black lines.
Fold along the dotted lines to
make some funny faces.

God knows
when I'm feeling
sad.

My
name

Nehemiah
1–3

# God knows when I'm feeling shy or scared.

Cut along the lines to make three smaller pages. Read the prayer words and draw a picture on each page. Make holes where shown and tie together with ribbon to make your own prayer book.

My name

Judges 6—8

Dear God,
When I'm feeling sad,
Thank you for keeping me safe.

When I'm feeling all alone,
Thank you for keeping me safe.

When I am feeling scared,
Thank you for keeping me safe always.

# Busy Hezekiah

2 Kings 18;19; 20:20–21

no limit

## Imaginative play

*You will need: simple props for 'busy' play.*

Set up home area and provide items such as brooms, dusters, pots and pans, aprons, pegs, clothes, an improvised washing-line. (Keep this to the side of the area, to avoid children getting tangled up in it.) Children delight in really washing and drying dishes if you have a suitable play area and waterproof aprons to protect clothing. Or improvise a shop, with a counter, a 'till', shopping bags, items to buy, play money and some dressing-up clothes (for boys as well as girls).

## Pouring water

*You will need: two small clear plastic jugs on a tray, with water in one; an absorbent cloth.*

Children try to pour water from one jug to the other without spilling. Top up the jug when necessary and don't fuss about spills: the idea is to practise pouring. The children can easily become anxious if they feel they are doing something 'wrong'.

## Cleaning silver

*You will need: some tarnished silverware, cleaning wipes and polishing cloths.*

Show the children how to polish and let them clean the silver items. The children will need to wash their hands thoroughly in soapy water after this activity.

## Preparing a snack

*You will need: a variety of sandwich spreads, butter, plastic knives and plates, plastic cups and a plastic jug of cool drink. Check for food allergies before you start and be alert to hygiene and safety standards.*

Children can make, eat and enjoy their own snacks! Encourage children to lay the table with cloth and serviettes.

Game time

10-15 mins

## Change!

Provide a few simple physical activities, eg jumping into and out of hoops on the floor, throwing beanbags into a bowl, throwing soft balls to one another, building a tower of blocks. Arrange children in small groups so that each starts at a different activity. When the children hear your signal (a bell or whistle) they must stop and move to the next activity. Change the activities briskly. After a few minutes ask if they like changing the activities so much. Chat about feeling frustrated if we are too busy. Allow children some time to pursue some of the activities.

## Under the cup

Have a different small object hidden under each of six upside down plastic cups, each one with a symbol drawn on it. Prepare a large sponge dice with the same symbols on the sides. The children throw the dice and must try to remember what is underneath the cup with the corresponding symbol.

20-30 mins

## Puppet making

*You will need: paper bags, wooden spoons, glue, buttons, coloured paper, cut wool, and fabric scraps to make features and clothes!*

Use the paper bags or spoons as the basis for making puppets. The children should glue on the other items as they wish. Encourage children to create their own puppets and invent their own characters. They may wish to develop their own plays with their puppets.

## Sewing

*You will need: card (the sides of cereal boxes work well), yarn, chenille wires, pens or crayons.*

Prepare pieces of card by punching holes around the perimeter. Fold a chenille wire in half and attach a length of brightly coloured wool. Fasten the other end of the wool to the box. The child can use the wire as a needle and sew the wool through the holes. When the sewing is completed the child uses felt-tip pens or broad wax crayons to draw a picture in the centre.

Story time

10 mins

## Busy Hezekiah

*Start by asking the children if they have had a busy time so far today. Chat about what they have been doing. Tell children that sometimes we say 'as busy as a bee' because bees are always working. Ask the children to 'buzz their fingers like bees' every time they hear the word 'busy' in the story.*

*This story is called 'Busy Hezekiah'. Did you remember to 'buzz your fingers'?*

Today I'm going to tell you about a very busy king. His name was Hezekiah. Hezekiah was busy, busy, busy all his life because he loved God and he wanted to be a good king.

Hezekiah was a young strong man when he first became king. Even when he was young he was very busy. He worked hard to show people that they must love God and pray to God.

Hezekiah was soon king over many lands. And still he was busy, busy, busy.

Some people tried to fight him – but God was on his side because Hezekiah loved God and listened to God.

Hezekiah even did a very clever thing. Some of his enemies tried to stop him getting water from the river. So Hezekiah kept his men busy digging a deep, deep tunnel under the ground, all the way down to the river. So he could get water without his enemy even knowing.

It was such a big tunnel that it's still there today! You can walk in it if you go to the country where he lived which is called Israel.

Hezekiah helped the people grow good food to eat. That kept them very busy too. Hezekiah did lots and lots of things. He was always busy. But the most important thing he did was to remember to follow God! Even when he was very busy Hezekiah remembered that it's important to talk with God.

*End by chatting about the busy things that the children like to do. Remind them of busy Hezekiah and how he still remembered to talk with God. Tell them they can always talk to God, no matter what they are busy doing!*

## Rhyme time

 **3-10 mins**

### Hezekiah

*This rhyme reminds us of what sorts of things busy Hezekiah did. If necessary, tell the children what a 'mole' is – both the animal and the excavator named after it! Hezekiah was like both!*

Hezekiah was busy – busy all the day,
He worked and worked and
    he liked to pray.

He chased away the enemies and dug
    a great big hole,
He dug through the ground
    like a great big mole!

Hezekiah was busy – busy all the day,
He worked and worked and
    he liked to pray.

He helped the people to grow good food,
To listen to God –
    he'll keep us safe.

Hezekiah was busy – busy all the day,
He worked and worked and
    he liked to pray.

## Song time

   **5 mins**

### Busy me
*Sing this song to the tune of 'I feel pretty'.*

I am busy, oh so busy,
    I'm as busy as busy can be,
I am busy, I'm as busy as a busy bee.

*Ask the children for suggestions of busy things which they can do. Repeat the words whilst miming appropriate actions.*

*Encourage children to create 'busy' words to the tune of 'Here we go round the mulberry bush', eg,*

This is the way we wash our clothes,
Wash our clothes,
Wash our clothes,
This is the way we wash our clothes,
Early in the morning.

## Pray time

    **3-5 mins**

### Busy bodies
*Talk about the different parts of our bodies we use when we are busy. With each suggestion that a child makes, ask the children to touch that part of their bodies and to pray after you a short 'thank you' for that body part, eg 'Thank you Lord for my hands that can hold cups and plates. Thank you Lord for my nose, which tells me when the food is cooking.'*

From *LACH*: 'Hello God it's me' and 'Move it!' p88, 'Playing' p87.

## Extra time

•Necklaces: colour pasta tubes with food colouring and use these for threading necklaces.

•Play dough hands: pre-cut hand shapes out of firm soft plastic. Give each child a hand and brightly coloured play dough. They enjoy creating bracelets, rings, etc, to decorate the hand!

•Scrapbook: create a group scrapbook of pictures of busy people.

•Busy growers: pre-soak bean seeds and help child plant the bean seed on a dish,

between layers of damp cotton wool.

•Watch a nature video clip of honey bees or watch a real bee busily gathering nectar.

## Adults too

Chat about how easy it is for us to feel impatient and want to do things ourselves rather than wait for our little ones to do it themselves. Ask for suggestions of the sort of situations where adults find it difficult to be patient, eg baby trying to feed himself, pre-schooler trying to tie their own shoelaces. We help our children develop self-esteem when they can announce, 'I can!' We need to try to focus on our long-term goal of raising confident, competent people. Perhaps we would find it easier to be patient with them learning to do new tasks if we took time off to nurture ourselves. Children learn more easily when we are relaxed and offering affirmation! Share ideas of what we can do to give ourselves 'special time', maybe have a cup of coffee out with spouse or good friend, treat ourselves to a massage or a bubble bath. Carers often feel almost guilty at spending time on themselves – but that is 'caring' too! Can you build up a list of reliable babysitters to make this more feasible for busy people?

*Just a Minute* by Christine Orme, SU, helps busy mums find time to spend with God.

## Top tip

Val says, 'Arrange for someone with a disability to visit the group and show the children how they manage with their challenge. For example, we had a blind woman visit our nursery school and show the children the special games she had, which she then taught the children to play. The children were also intrigued with her Braille watch and her sock holder (for keeping pairs of socks together in the wash and in the drawer).'

**ACTIVITY PAGE:**
**The photocopiable activity page for this outline is on page 88**

2 Kings
18;19;
20:20–21

## Thank you God that we can be busy with our hands.

Put your hands on your head,
Put your hands on your nose,
Put your hands on your head,
Put your hands on your toes.
Put your hands on your lips,
Put your hands in the air.
Put your hands on your shoe,
Put your hands right behind.
Here are my hands to use, Lord,
Please help me to be kind.

My
name

Make patterns with
your hands all
round the page.
Use finger paints or
draw round your
hand with a crayon.

# First steps in Bible reading
## The *Tiddlywinks* range of Little Books

**My Little Red Book**
*First steps in Bible reading*
Reese discovers Christmas is coming...
978 1 85999 659 1

**My Little Yellow Book**
*First steps in Bible reading*
Danny finds out about Easter.
978 1 85999 693 5

**My Little Blue Book**
*First steps in Bible reading*
Lucy and Liam find out All about me...
978 1 85999 660 7

**My Little Green Book**
*First steps in Bible reading*
Krista explores God's wonderful world
978 1 85999 696 6

**My Little Purple Book**
*First steps in Bible reading*
Lily discovers 'Jesus loves me'
978 1 85999 720 8

**My Little Orange Book**
*First steps in Bible reading*
Jamie looks inside God's big book.
978 1 85999 717 8

*Tiddlywinks* Little Books are designed to be used at home by a parent/carer with an individual child. Linked to the themes covered in the *Tiddlywinks* Big Books, children can discover and learn about the Bible and share their discoveries with you. There are 50 first steps in Bible reading pages in each book, with a story for each day and extra activity pages of fun things to do. Children will love exploring the Bible with child characters Lucy and Liam, Reese, Danny and Krista.
A5, 64pp £3.99 each

You can order these or any other *Tiddlywinks* resources from:
● Your local Christian bookstore
● Scripture Union Mail Order:
  Telephone 01908 856006
● Online: log on to
  **www.scriptureunion.org.uk/shop**
to order securely from our online bookshop

66 *When the Big Books are used in conjunction with the Little Books, children and adults encounter an attractive mixture of stories and activities that will encourage everybody to know and trust in Jesus.*
**Diana Turner,**
**Editor of *Playleader Magazine*** 99

### Tiddlywinks
*The flexible resource for pre-school children and carers*

### Also now on sale!
*Glitter and Glue. Say and Sing*
*Even more craft and prayer ideas for use with under fives*

89

# Harvest special

**Genesis 8:22**

*Celebrate God's world and the wonders of harvest with this half-day event, especially for young children and with plenty to involve their parents, carers and families too.*

## Through the farm gate

As people arrive, involve them in making a big group poster with the message 'It's harvest time' in huge letters on a sturdy background. Decorate with:

•potato prints,

•children's drawings of fruits and vegetables, cut out and glued on,

•magazine pictures of food,

•cover the letters with lentils, pasta, dried beans, dried fruit, pot pourri glued on with PVA,

•straw, hay, wheat or barley can be put round the edges as a frame.

Work on the poster during the event: children who find the excitement too much will enjoy a less demanding occupation.

### Around the farm

Run activity areas concurrently; or, with limited space and numbers, do one activity at a time. Decorate each area with coloured flags and streamers. Devise a running-order that suits your group, venue and timescale (see chart example).

### All together

Plan two other areas for joint activities.

## Around the farm

### FIELD FUN

#### Sand play
*You will need: sand tray(s); tractors; toy farm equipment; plastic farm animals; sand hats; aprons; dustpan and brush.*

Protect the children's hair and clothes. Allow free play with the sand – for the adults too!

And make sweeping up at the end all part of the fun!

#### Farm play
*You will need: farm animal masks, farmer's hat, boots; posters and books about farming.*

Talk to the children about life on a farm: be realistic! Use posters and books to find out more. Discover whether a sheepdog is a pet, where eggs and milk come from, how we get wool from sheep – and more!

Allow the children to play freely at being farmers and animals. Improvise a game where a few children work as sheepdogs and guide the 'sheep' into a pen made from chairs.

### PADDOCK PLAY

#### Help the Farmer obstacle 'race'
*Set up a fun obstacle course. For instance:*

•put potatoes in a sack,

•collect up leaves and place in a bag,

•place fruit from pretend trees in a basket,

•put on the farmer's hat and boots.

Demonstrate to the children how to play the game. Encourage everyone to applaud once a child finishes the route.

#### The farmer's in his den
Enjoy playing the traditional nursery game. Remind the children to be gentle as they pat the bone!

### ORCHARD ANTICS

Children will need to wear aprons and wash hands before and after the activity. Be alert about safety and hygiene; check about food allergies before you start.

#### Fruit and veg
*You will need: a cutting board; knife; large transparent plastic bowl; small bowls and spoons and ingredients to make either – fruit salad: variety of seasonal fruits; fruit juice – or coleslaw: one quarter white cabbage; small onion; large carrot; dessert apple; salad cream or mayonnaise.*

Look together at the fruit or vegetables. Cut one item and talk about how it looks. Show children how to cut it into pieces. Allow one child at a time to help you cut small pieces (safety is a priority!) Put all the chopped pieces in a big bowl and stir well with juice (fruit salad) or salad cream (coleslaw). Serve small portions for children to sample.

### GARDEN GROWERS

Everyone will need to wear protective clothing and to wash their hands thoroughly afterwards.

#### Growing cress
*You will need: damp tissue, cress seeds, plastic trays or flat tubs.*

Talk to the children about what the seeds need to grow. Place the damp tissue and seeds in the tubs. (Decorating tubs or flowerpots can be an extra activity. Or use half-eggshells with faces drawn on.) Label each tub with the child's name.

#### Nasturtiums
*You will need: nasturtium seeds, small plant pots, compost, spoons.*

Spoon some compost into a pot. Press three or four seeds into the compost and cover over. Remind the children that when they take the seeds home they will need light and water to grow. Nasturtiums are bright to look at – and you can safely eat the flowers and leaves.

### Around the farm

| Area | Activities | Colour |
|------|-----------|--------|
| FIELD FUN | Sand play; farm play | Brown |
| PADDOCK PLAY | Obstacle race; farmer's den | Yellow |
| ORCHARD ANTICS | Fruit salad; coleslaw | Orange |
| GARDEN GROWERS | Growing plants | Green |

### All together

| | |
|---|---|
| Down in the meadow | Story drama, songs, rhymes, prayer |
| Grazing land | Harvest 'supper |

## Together times

### Down in the meadow
Practise the story script beforehand so

you can lead confidently. It needs no rehearsal by the children. (Making animal headbands or masks could be an extra craft activity.)

Make a display table of fruit and vegetables, things made or prepared today and any harvest gifts. Place it where everyone can see it.

Sing along and improvise actions to a recording of 'We plough the fields and scatter'. Or chant this rhyme, to your own tune as you all dance around:

> Yummy, yummy apples so red
> Yummy, yummy we will be fed
> It's harvest, it's harvest
> We've all been fed!
>
> Crunchy, crunchy gooseberries green
> Crunchy, crunchy – best you've seen
> It's harvest, it's harvest
> The best you've ever seen!

Say some traditional rhymes which both adults and children will know: 'Oats and beans and barley grow'; 'Lavender's blue'. Introduce this new rhyme.

> Red beans, blackberries, gooseberries
> Bright and green.
> All for harvest –
> The best you've ever seen!
>
> Green beans, yellow bananas,
> Apples so red –
> All for harvest –
> You will be fed!
>
> Potatoes, carrots,
> Nice cabbage white,
> All for harvest,
> The best – oh what a sight!

### Mr Farmer's harvest time

*Involve all the children (and enthusiastic adults) in the following story. You will need boots for the Farmers; everyone else needs a simple headband with ears to identify their role. When the children hear their animal mentioned, they stand up, walk around the 'farmyard' and sit down again. (Ask some adult helpers to guide this.) Choose two confident children to be Mr and Mrs Farmer; divide the remainder into chickens, pigs, cows, and sheep.*

Mr Farmer woke up one bright and sunny morning. He yawned and said, 'I have so much to do because it's harvest time. I don't know how I'm going to get it all done by myself.' He shook his head, got dressed and went down stairs.

'Good morning dear,' said Mrs Farmer. 'It's harvest time. Isn't that wonderful?'

'Yes, it is wonderful, but how am I going to get all my work done?' said Mr Farmer shaking his head sadly.

'I can help!' said Mrs Farmer. 'Just you wait and see. We will get it all done.'

After breakfast Mr and Mrs Farmer went down into the farmyard to check on all the animals.

'Good morning,' clucked the chickens. 'Isn't it wonderful! It's harvest time!'

'Yes,' said Mr Farmer. 'It is wonderful, but how am I going to get all my work done?' And he shook his head sadly.

'We can help!' clucked the chickens. 'Just you wait and see. We will get it all done.'

So, Mr and Mrs Farmer and the chickens walked around the farmyard helping get the work done. They collected the eggs and put them in a basket. They went to see the pigs.

'Good morning,' snuffled the pigs. 'Isn't it wonderful! It's harvest time!'

'Yes,' said Mr Farmer. 'It is wonderful, but how am I going to get all my work done?' And he shook his head sadly.

'We can help!' snuffled the pigs. 'Just you wait and see. We will get it all done.'

So, Mr and Mrs Farmer, the chickens and the pigs walked around the farmyard helping get the work done. They dug up the potatoes and they put them in the sacks. They went to see the cows.

'Good morning,' mooed the cows. 'Isn't it wonderful. It's harvest time!'

'Yes,' said Mr Farmer. 'It is wonderful but how am I going to get all my work done?' And he shook his head sadly.

'We can help!' mooed the cows. 'Just you wait and see. We will get it all done.'

So, Mr and Mrs Farmer, the chickens, the pigs and the cows walked around the farmyard helping get the work done. They collected the milk from the cows. They went to see the sheep.

'Good morning,' baaed the sheep. 'Isn't it wonderful! It's harvest time!'

'Yes,' said Mr Farmer. 'It is wonderful, but how am I going to get all my work done?' And he shook his head sadly.

'We can help,' baaed the sheep. 'Just you wait and see. We will get it all done.'

So, Mr and Mrs Farmer, the chickens, the pigs, the cows and the sheep walked around the farmyard helping get the work done. They gathered the wool from the sheep and put it into bags. They all worked very hard.

'I must gather in all the fruit and vegetables. And cut the wheat field. And I mustn't forget the bales of hay to be put in the barns. Oh dear, how will I get everything ready in time?' said Mr Farmer, shaking his head.

Mrs Farmer, the chickens, the pigs, the cows and the sheep all laughed. 'Look!' they said. 'We have all helped each other and we have got the work done!'

Mr Farmer laughed too. 'Thank you,' he said!

## Pray time

*End with a prayer which brings in many elements of your time together. Explain that you are going to talk to God but you want everyone to keep their eyes open to see what you are telling him about. Point to the items on your display and create your own prayer based on this one:*

Dear Father God,
Thank you for harvest time.
Thank you for apples.
Thank you for cress.
Thank you for fruit salad.
*(Continue naming things from your display.)*
Thank you for all the good things you have given us,                Amen.

## Grazing land

### Harvest 'supper'

Eating together is a traditional way of celebrating harvest. Try giving the meal a theme:

Picnic party: individual picnic meals in food bags; add a boxed drink. If the weather isn't kind, enjoy an indoor picnic.

Bring-and-share: plan this beforehand and ask people for specific items so you get a good variety.

Colour co-ordinated: have as much of the food as possible in a chosen colour! All wear the same shade too!

Scare the crows: wear baggy clothes and hats with straw, or dungarees and boots.

# Welcome time

The beginning of a session is a busy time, with everyone arriving, meeting up with friends, freeing children from the constraints of car seat or buggy, or setting out equipment, preparing refreshments and maybe taking money. But greeting the children and the adults who bring them is a time when you can really make them welcome in a special way. The ideas given on these pages aim to give you a structure for making that 'hello' an experience which affirms everyone in the group.

You could use a different welcome time idea each time you meet. Or select one which suits your group and use that to launch your time together every session. This will help build a sense of group identity so that even very young children will start to join in with a regular and repeated introduction. It will become the signal for the group to come together, to settle and to look forward to what is going to happen next.

Your group may have a fluid start time – if so, save your welcome for a time when the whole group comes together, maybe for some singing or a story, or before refreshments.

If you start at a set time, have an informal sing-song or news sharing for a few minutes before your regular welcome, so that stragglers have an opportunity to arrive and join in.

*Tiddlywinks: The Big Green Book* has ideas for welcoming everyone to your group plus extra ways of welcoming new children or visitors, saying a positive 'hello' to parents and carers, and for celebrating birthdays.

Turn to pages 94 and 95 for home time ideas.

There are more welcome time ideas in other 'Big Books' in the *Tiddlywinks* range.

## Welcome time idea 1

*Hello Teddy*

Sit the children in a circle facing inwards, preferably on a carpeted area. Introduce a teddy or other character toy and explain that the children may only speak when they are holding the teddy. Hold a pretend conversation with the cuddly toy, saying, 'Hello Teddy my name is (Denise).' Pass the teddy to the next child in the circle and prompt them to introduce themselves. It is important to let children know that they can simply pass Teddy on or whisper to him, if they don't want to talk out loud.

You can play 'Goodbye Teddy' too at Home time. As the teddy goes round the circle each person says, 'My name is (Denise) – goodbye, Teddy.'

Use a variation on this activity for any time when the children are feeling shy. Pass a toy puppy around the group whilst seated in a circle, say hello to him and stroke him.

## Welcome to adults

*Special people*

New people visiting or joining your group – adults and children – often need things fairly low-key to begin with. But they will appreciate their own 'special person' to show them around and answer any questions they may have. A friendly smile and a few words will make them feel welcomed without being overwhelmed. Young children will often stay with a parent or carer through the whole of a first session: don't try to push them into taking part until they are ready – they will be watching and absorbing what's going on at their own pace.

## Welcome time idea 2

*We belong*

This welcome chant is suitable for groups meeting in a church-based situation. It is easy to learn as everyone echoes the words of a leader. If you wish to use it as a song, the words will fit the tune of 'Frère Jacques'. Choose a verse or use them all. This idea can also be used at the end of your session.

Many people,
Many people,
All belong,
All belong,
To the Jesus family,
To the Jesus family,
Round the world,
Round the world.

All of us,
All of us,
Can belong,
Can belong,
To the Jesus family,
To the Jesus family,
Round the world,
Round the world.

Thank you, Jesus,
Thank you, Jesus,
We belong,
We belong,
To the Jesus family,
To the Jesus family,
Here and now,
Here and now.

## Welcome time idea

### 3

*Is that me?*

Inflate a balloon for each child and as they arrive invite them to come and watch as you draw a simple face on the balloon (with the knot at the top) and write their name on it. Tie some strands of wool around the knot as hair for the face. Using a piece of paper masking tape, let the child stick this to the wall until it is time to go home. During the session, pause and all look at the balloons and think about all the people in the group today. You could also use the balloons as a prayer focus, thanking God for each person shown.

## Welcome time idea

### 4

*Welcome everyone*

Welcome everybody with this rhyme or song, which goes to the tune of 'Humpty Dumpty'. (You will probably have to take liberties with the rhythm to fit in the children's names.)

Welcome, welcome, everyone here.
Welcome James and welcome Hayley,
Welcome Lee and welcome Martin.
We are glad you're here with us today.

## Welcome to new children or visitors

*Roll the ball*

All sit on the floor in a circle. Take a large soft ball and roll it across the circle to a particular child: as they catch it say 'Hello Sarah,' and ask everyone else to say hello to Sarah too. Sarah then rolls the ball back to you and you can repeat the process, until everyone has been welcomed. Use the child's name frequently during this game: it will sound artificial to you at first but it will help the child to focus on who is talking to them and to absorb some techniques of social interaction.

Variations on this game include:

The child who receives the ball rolls it to another child, rather than back to the leader.

After saying hello, you can ask one or two other questions or comment, eg 'It's Sarah's first time here today. I hope you have a fun time Sarah.'

## Happy Birthday

Decorate an airtight biscuit tin to resemble a cake, using fireproof materials. Fix five candleholders on the lid, so candles can be replaced easily and the correct number can be used for each child. Prepare the 'cake' for the birthday child: put a selection of biscuits, cookies or small cakes inside. (Avoid types which may include nuts and be aware of any other allergies.) Add the candles to the holders. Put the cake on a table.

Invite the child to come and stand by the table. Light the candles and have one helper whose job it is to keep an eye on them. Lead everyone in chanting and clapping out the rhythm of 'Ha-ppy - birth - day': repeat the greeting to match the age of the child. Let the child blow out the candles.

Carefully remove the lid (put it aside, well out of reach) and let the child take the container to everyone in the group so they can each choose a biscuit to enjoy. Make sure the child remembers to have one, too! This activity works well during a regular 'drinks' or refreshment time.

# Home time

The end of a session can be chaotic, with some people in a rush to leave, others still chattering, children tired and fractious or still full of energy and reluctant to be strapped into a buggy or to wear a coat. Leaders may be busy clearing up and cleaning up. But a positive home time can make each person – child and adult – feel they are valued and encourage them to come another time.

You could use a different home time idea each time you meet. Or select one which suits your group and use that to close your time together every session. This will help build a sense of group identity so that even very young children will start to join in with a regular and repeated 'goodbye'. It will help each member of the group to feel part of a community – even one which only lasts an hour – and to affirm each person there.

If you finish at a set time, select a home time activity to use as the last item of your programme. Make sure you allow enough time so that people don't feel they have to hurry off or miss this part.

If your group is less structured, choose a time when you are all together, towards the end of the session.

Make home time a definite event and avoid having people putting away equipment or clearing up at the same time: aim to include and involve everyone.

*Tiddlywinks: The Big Green Book* has ideas for saying 'goodbye' to everyone in your group plus extra ways of marking 'milestone' events: those going to a new area or leaving the group to start school.

Turn back to pages 92 and 93 for welcome time ideas.

There are more home time ideas in other 'Big Books' in the *Tiddlywinks* range.

## Home time idea 1

*Goodbye prayer*
This short prayer has a repeated line which children can memorise well and quickly. Use this at the end of a circle time together or at the end of a worship time, as a blessing prayer.

> As we say 'Goodbye',
> Go with us, Lord.
> As we leave this place,
> Go with us, Lord.
> In everything we do,
>     in the week ahead,
> Go with us, Lord.

## Home time idea 2

*Thanks for friends*
At the end of a session, it is good to think about what has been going on and how we have spent time together. Young children are developing concepts of friendship and this action rhyme gives some structure and words to express those early understandings. Choose a verse that seems most appropriate for your group or use the whole rhyme. Everyone will be able to join in the last lines.

> Friends can walk together,
> *(Walk fingers along.)*
> Laugh and talk together,
> *(Smile and 'talk' with hands.)*
> **Thanks for friends!**
>
> Friends can cry together,
> *(Look sad and mime crying.)*
> Have great fun together,
> *(Dance fingers about.)*
> **Thanks for friends!**
>
> Friends can stay together,
> *(Link forefingers.)*
> Sing and pray together,
> *(Hands together.)*
> **Thanks for friends!**

## Going to school

*Who'll go to school?*
This game works well where you have a number of children who will be starting school soon. Use the tune and method of 'Oranges and lemons' to sort the children into those who are moving on and those who will stay in the group a while longer. You could play this for several sessions to get the children used to the idea of changing.

Two leaders make an arch. The children move in a snakey line under the arch singing:

> We're all together, we're playing a game.
> Everyone's different, there's no one the same.
> Soon it will be time to make a new start.
> Soon it will be time when we have to part.
> Who'll go to school, or who will stay?
> Let's find out soon, let's see today.

As the adults make the 'chopping action' they say 'Here, there, here, there…' and stop at appropriate 'chop' for right child each time. School children line up behind one leader and those staying, behind the other. (With such young children, do not have a tug of war at the end of the game.)

### Home time idea

**3**

*Thank you God*

This quieter rhyme has a second verse which everyone can say together, with a leader speaking the first section. Use the rhyme while sitting or standing together holding hands in a circle, to reinforce the togetherness of the words.

> When we're happy, when we're glad
> Or when we're feeling rather sad,
> Thank you, thank you, thank you God
> For looking after us.
>
> Thank you, thank you, thank you God!
> Thank you, thank you, thank you God!
> Thank you, thank you, thank you God
> For looking after us.

### Home time idea

**4**

*Sing and shout*

With plenty of space and no limit on sound pollution, enjoy this song and dance for a noisy send off. Stand in a circle or in a space and sing to the tune of the 'Hokey cokey'. Repeat with left arm, right leg, left leg, whole self. Or use 'first arm', 'other arm', etc, for young children who are not yet certain of their right and left. The traditional 'holding hands and going into the centre of the circle' takes a lot of organising and unravelling with very little children: instead, let them improvise their own dances on the spot.

> You put your right (or 'first') arm in,
> Your right arm out.
> In, out, in, out,
> Shake it all about.
> Remember God is with us
> And there is no doubt.
> That's why we sing and shout!
> Oh, dance to God our father,
> Oh, dance to God our father,
> Oh, dance to God our father,
> Everyone sing and shout!

### Get Ready Go

A child's first day at school is a big moment for them... and you. But while some children can't wait to get started, others might not be so confident. Making sure your children are ready to go is really important.

*Get Ready Go!* is a brilliant new book for children about to start primary school. Using simple words, bright pictures and fun activities, *Get Ready Go!* explains what school is going to be like, helping your children prepare for that exciting first term.

*Get Ready Go!* comes complete with a companion guide for parents, packed with useful advice so that you can help them get ready too.

*Get Ready Go!* is a great new resource for all Early Years educators and can also be used by primary schools as a central part of their induction programme.

A colourful two book set available singly or in packs of 5. Each set contains:

### Get Ready to Let Go

'Have I put enough in her lunchbox?' Essential preparation for families and parents.

### Get Ready Go!

'What's it going to be like?' A clear, friendly guide to help children talk and think about the big adventure of starting school!

Individual set – £2.99 ISBN 978 1 84427 132 0

Pack of 5 – £10.00 ISBN 978 1 84427 133 7

### Moving away

One of your 'families' is leaving the group and moving on. If they are moving house, they are not going to want more to take with them, but you may still want to mark their going. How about arranging a farewell lunch for them? Choose (and book if necessary) a venue nearby which welcomes young children (has suitable menu, seating and play facilities). After your usual meeting or on another agreed date, have a meal together. Enjoy a social event where the children are catered for as well as the adults. Pay for your own meals and either use group funds or each put in a bit extra for your 'farewell family'. Take a few photos so they have a memento of the occasion.

# Have you enjoyed this book?

Then take a look at the other Big Books in the *Tiddlywinks* range. Why not try them all?

**The Big Orange Book**
Themes: What's inside God's big book? All creatures great and small; Friends of God; Stories of Jesus
978 1 85999 716 1

**The Big Red Book**
Themes: Christmas is coming; People we meet; Stories Jesus told; God gives us food
978 1 85999 658 4

**The Big Blue Book**
Themes: All about me; God gives us... homes, clothes, food, etc; People who knew Jesus; Friends of God
978 1 85999 657 7

**The Big Yellow Book**
Themes: Easter; God gives us families; Friends of Jesus; What's the weather like?
978 1 85999 692 8

**The Big Purple Book**
Themes: Jesus love me; God love it when I... make music, sing, dance, look at books, I'm 'me'; Friends and followers; Materials and technology
978 1 85999 719 2

**The Big Green Book**
Themes: God's wonderful world; God gives us people; Let's find out about Jesus; God knows when I'm... happy, cross, sad, scared, busy
978 1 85999 695 9

'I love this! It's great!' Sarah, leader of a 3 to 5s group in Victoria, Australia.

Tiddlywinks Big Books are designed for use in any pre-school setting. The multi-purpose outlines are packed full of play, prayers, crafts, stories and rhymes; simply pick and mix ideas to meet the particular needs of your group. You'll find plenty of practical advice on setting up and running a pre-school group, plus ideas in every session to help you include adult carers. The children will love the illustrated activity pages.

A4, 96pp, £11.99 each

You can order these or any other *Tiddlywinks* resources from:

- Your local Christian bookstore
- Scripture Union Mail Order: Telephone 01908 856006
- Online: log on to **www.scriptureunion.org.uk/shop** to order securely from our online bookshop

'...really pleased with your material and look forward to integrating Tiddlywinks into our existing programme.' Marion, Scotland

**The flexible resource for pre-school children and carers**

### Also now on sale!

*Glitter and Glue. Say and Sing.*
*Even more craft and prayer ideas for use with under fives*